The Once and Future Park

Essays by

Herbert Muschamp

Sam Bass Warner, Jr.

Patricia Phillips

Edward Ball

Diana Balmori

Princeton Architectural Press

Published in the United States of America by Princeton Architectural Press, Inc., 37 East 7th Street, New York, New York 10003.

Editors: Deborah Karasov and Steve Waryan
Designer: Kristen McDougall
Editor, Walker Art Center: Phil Freshman

This book was typeset on a Macintosh II with Quark XPress using DIN Mittelschrift and DIN Neuzit Grotesk bold condensed typefaces. It was printed on Mowhawk Superfine paper by Friesen Printers, Altona, Manitoba.

Library of Congress Cataloguing-in-Publication Data

The Once and future park / essays by Herbert Muschamp . . . [et al.]. — 1st ed.
    p. cm.
    Based on a symposium and exhibition cosponsored by the Walker Art Center and the Minneapolis College of Art and Design in the spring of 1992.
    Includes bibliographical references.
    ISBN 1-878271-76-8 (paper) : $19.95
    1. Parks—Congresses. 2. Parks—United States—Congresses.
3. Parks—Designs and plans—Exhibitions. I. Muschamp, Herbert.
II. Walker Art Center. III. Minneapolis College of Art and Design.
SB481.A2053 1993
712 .5—dc20   93-40464
                                                         CIP

Funding for The Once and Future Park symposium and exhibition was provided by the National Endowment for the Arts. Support for the Minneapolis College of Art and Design exhibition program is provided by the Northwest Area Foundation.

opposite: Logan neighborhood park, Minneapolis, at the turn of the century.
overleaf: View of Lake Calhoun, Minneapolis, early twentieth century.

Printed in Canada

Contents

Foreword

Kathy Halbreich

This book is a series of essays and speculative project statements that propose the park as an ideal site for exploring the relationship between culture and nature. The authors, who variously cover the fields of history, ecology, art, and landscape architecture, argue that parks should play a greater role in our lives and offer their notions about the nature of public space in general.

Rarely do American parks reflect the sweeping social changes that have taken place in our time, nor are they designed or programmed inventively. However, if imaginatively reshaped, our parks could provide fertile experimental ground for a variety of artists and social critics and leaders. These include cultural critics who call for public projects that mirror a range of community values; ecologists, designers, and visual artists who are trying to enlarge the possibilities of cross-disciplinary design; and civic leaders who are interested in new partnerships that expand the park's function in the life of their cities.

The book grew out of an exhibition and related symposium that were collaboratively organized by the Walker Art Center and the Minneapolis College of Art and Design's MCAD Gallery. We are extremely grateful to the staff of the college, especially Julie Yanson, who curated the <u>Once and Future Park</u> exhibition, and to the National Endowment for the Arts for its financial support. The symposium was held, in part, in anticipation of the September 1992 dedication of the expansion of the Minneapolis Sculpture Garden, which is the product of a unique, continuing partnership between the Walker and the Minneapolis Park and Recreation Board. Now eleven acres in all and containing some forty works, the Garden is the largest urban sculpture park in the nation. Since the first section of the Garden opened, in September 1988, it has been visited by more than one million people. The Walker-Park and Recreation Board partnership has been a significant and productive one. For example, the Board uses the Garden as a site for its summer-employment program for at-risk youth, employing teens as tour guides. In addition to containing art installations both permanent and temporary, the Garden serves as a community-based site, with programs ranging from performances to family art workshops to community art parades to literary readings. Funded primarily from private sources, the Minneapolis Sculpture Garden is a vibrant example of the role parks can play in the revitalizing of public culture.

KATHY HALBREICH IS THE DIRECTOR OF THE WALKER ART CENTER.

Introduction
Deborah Karasov

Frogtown in St. Paul, Minnesota, is a depressed, often over-looked neighborhood of single-family homes bounded on the north by railroad yards and on the south by the cluttered commercial strip of University Avenue. Vacant lots, for-sale signs, and chain-link fences are common components of the landscape. The only public park in the neighborhood is a rectangular grassy space with corner baseball diamonds, a few randomly placed benches, and a typical toddler play area. A large, ungainly structure, nearly windowless, sprawls at the end of a short path from the parking lot. Inside this "community center" a narrow corridor strings together a series of rooms that include a small video arcade and a gymnasium.

In this Frogtown park, and duplicated in many parks of more affluent neighborhoods around the country, are the remnants of different municipal park movements, ranging from the picturesque landscapes of the late nineteenth century to the recreational and reform facilities of the early twentieth. These disparate elements—trees, grass, building, and path—arranged onto a section of land like pieces of assorted board games, fulfill their individual functions but symbolize how they no longer add up to a meaningful design.

During a 1992 urban-design study for St. Paul, sponsored by a nonprofit public art organization, the participants decided that Frogtown needed parks that were more accessible and visible. Within months, the St. Paul Companies, a private Twin Cities corporation, provided funds for seven high school students, guided by Minnesota-based artist Seitu Jones, to create a different kind of park on one of Frogtown's vacant lots. Traditional parks stand in contrast to the surrounding city because of their naturalistic landscaping. But in Frogtown's new park, color will provide the contrast. A multi-colored hopscotch sidewalk, a maze of colored stone, and a basketball court, emblazoned with a frog in basketball shoes "skying" for the hoop, will contrast with the drab homes of the neighborhood. A line made up of wooden houselike facades—with solid colors on one side, vibrant murals on the other—will mimic the scale and shape of the surrounding homes and form a gateway to the park.

New kinds of parks like this one are important if we are to counteract a growing problem with our existing parks.

opposite: The characteristic American park today is made up of a functional but un-imaginative and incoherent assortment of recreational and landscape features.

Most American parks have been perceived through the nineteenth-century Olmstedian model of pastoral landscape set in an urban context—a model still followed by the majority of park designers—with its elements, in post-World War II years, increasingly reduced to trivial size and cut up by recreational facilities. Such parks are fine individually and hardly need to be done away with. But, overall, parks have failed to keep up with our increasingly complex cultural needs.

This book takes as its starting point the idea that customary models for park design are no longer adequate. Its five coauthors believe that there are critical ecological, educational, and artistic roles parks could and should be playing, both today and in the coming century. In short, the basic notion of "park" is in great need of being rethought.

The consequences of not rethinking parks, I believe, would be alarming. Perhaps the most profound such consequence would be the lost opportunity to address ecological issues. Indeed, as Herbert Muschamp writes in this book, the urban park may provide the most readily available site for reconfiguring the relationship between nature and culture. Perhaps, rather than expressing a naive attitude toward a peaceable nature, an attitude that is more than one hundred years old, parks could educate our children about the change, decay, and disorder that affect the environment today. Ironically, although many designers have claimed to be formally inspired by the "earth art" of the artist Robert Smithson, few have thought about its sources—Smithson's reflections on a landscape corroded by the intensification of human intervention. Moreover, park designers must also begin to realize that they should share in the effort to recycle water and land, a call sounded clearly by Diana Balmori in her essay. As devastated places such as abandoned industrial sites, depleted quarries, and polluted lakes and rivers increasingly become available for public use, designers will have the great opportunity to rehabilitate spaces as much as plan them.

We must also rethink parks in terms of how they do or do not respond to the increasing homogeneity of our environmental experiences. To counter this trend, as Patricia Phillips shows in writing favorably about Arizona's Papago Park, designers could find provocative ideas for aesthetically rich parks by drawing from the surrounding landscape. Urban children are not the only ones who encounter prosaic

DEBORAH KARASOV, TRAINED AS A LANDSCAPE ARCHITECT AND CULTURAL GEOGRAPHER, IS THE HEAD OF ADULT EDUCATION PROGRAMS AT THE WALKER ART CENTER.

and indistinguishable parks. Today's suburban children—who represent the majority of children in the United States—experience nearly identical landscapes, regardless of the region or ecological zone in which they live. The vistas they encounter are made up of grass-lined freeways and for-sale signs rising out of bean fields; the largest open areas they typically see are a hodgepodge of golf courses, swimming beaches, playgrounds, and picnic areas strung out along paved roads. Rather than adding to this monotony, parks could—and a few already do—artistically express a variety of spatial and visual experiences: the open rural landscape, say, or the elegant rows of trees that serve as windbreaks, or the abutment of forest and field, or even, as in Papago Park, the marking of celestial events.

There are compelling reasons, therefore, why we must reinterpret the park for the cultural needs of our time. The first step, though, is to understand how creating parks today is different from in the past. One hundred years ago, as Sam Bass Warner explains here, reformers were able to propose large pastoral parks bought with ample public money as a solution to the environmental crises of that time, overcrowding and disease. Large tracts of cheap land were then readily available to be transformed into curvilinear vistas and picturesque compositions, the perfect design solutions for conjoining the vast emptiness of wilderness with the confinement of the city.

Today, untouched land is scarce and public projects are subsidized by private funds, making it harder to effect a grand public gesture. This is true even in our rapidly developing exurbs, where some residents naively assume that the open meadows meeting the defined edges of their backyards will be there forever. Rather than countering the decaying effects of the city, "nature" has become a place where urban and natural-resource economies meet in commercial ventures such as nature films, tourism, and the forestry and mining industries.

Further complicating the picture is the fact that our expectations for public life have also changed greatly since the prototypical American parks were created. While some park users stroll along the paths and sit quietly among the manicured gardens—the image of bourgeois leisure to which nineteenth-century reformers hoped everyone would aspire—others feel just as comfortable using parks as places to fix their cars, dance to music, or just hang out. That some feel such behavior is misbehavior reflects a deficiency in the variety of parks we have today and in the ways park designers have thought about them.

Not only parks but many other forms of public-space design will be challenged by such late twentieth-century developments as insufficient public financing, a conflicted relationship with nature, and a generally segregated public life. By moving to embrace these challenges, however, public parks can serve as extraordinary laboratories for bringing far-reaching, even seemingly unresolvable issues into coherent relationship with one another. And, exposing our often ambiguous notions of <u>nature</u> and <u>public</u> may be as innovative a source for design as resolving them. As Herbert Muschamp contends, parks can be meeting grounds for diverse ways of thinking and for new approaches to design—experiments in cultural as well as environmental ecology.

As suggested, this book grew from a recognition of the need to reimagine the role of the park. Revealing valuable possibilities, the authors confront the changes that have also occurred in the financing of parks and in our understanding of public life and the environment. Edward Ball, for instance, argues that our park designs should have a more ironic and critical edge, in order to combat the trivializing effects of theme parks. There are other examples of such conceits. We cannot make our designs more profound, for example, by simply using a new contrivance, like the trend of designing-by-metaphor, in which it seems every walkway represents a "Path through Chaos" and every skewed axis symbolizes "Society Unhinged."

Unfortunately, many design schools, especially landscape architecture departments, still teach the design process to future design professionals as if it were a rarified endeavor. The myth persists that landscape designs can be treated as isolated problems, similar to the way many architects design buildings without regard to the urban system surrounding them. Furthermore, design studios—the arenas in which the sacraments of the profession are exhaustively, and exhaustingly, taught—are rarely places of intellectual collaboration. In such domains, complex economic and cultural issues are often arrogantly simplified.

Yet we have reason to be optimistic. The authors here contend that significant innovation will come from a change in the way we design public space—from new models for collaboration among the professions involved in the design process. Then, visual form can be based on a serious investigation into our community and our natural systems.

In addition to the essays, this book contains statements by those whose work was included in the exhibition The Once and Future Park. Emerging Midwestern designers were invited to speculate on various social and aesthetic issues related to park design; the second part of the book presents their ideas. The variety displayed in their work reflects one strength of design schools today: for all their foibles, these schools do stimulate an important artistic plurality. But design schools need to teach students how to develop and refine their rough ideas, and to instruct them in the subtle art of collaboration.

In our current park predicament, where there are no easy design precedents and where designs are often lacking in new approaches, artistic experimentation is vital. To return to Frogtown, it is certain that the new park being created there will not remake the neighborhood's image, much less upgrade its economic condition. Moreover, there are circumstances that could mitigate its potential for success. For instance, prior to the inception of the project, an article in a local newspaper suggested that most of St. Paul's gangs originate in Frogtown, a charge that will probably shadow any neighborhood effort to enhance its image. Also, some designers may feel that the new park's plan has too much open lawn. Finally, it is possible that the teenagers designing the park's flower bed (another element of color in the scheme) will create a commonplace design instead of an imaginative one. Still, I have a sense that, in the end, this park will positively affect children's lives and reverberate with community value. Such a park need not replace our existing ones, or even the lavish downtown parks sometimes commissioned by city leaders, but it is an important complement for ensuring a diversified experience. We need, urgently, to imagine a range of environments that enrich our cultural life and reshape our link with nature.

Looking beyond Vision

Herbert Muschamp

Some years ago, the editor of a design publication asked me to contribute to a special issue on the subject of ecology. I was unable to accept his invitation but enthusiastically recommended a recently hired colleague, an architectural historian who, in recent years, has become an eloquent spokesperson for the environmental movement in New York City. No, no, the editor replied. That was exactly what he did not want. He was not planning to publish something sympathetic to environmental issues. On the contrary, he wanted to target the problem of what he termed "eco-fascism," a term that was new to me. Was I not alarmed about eco-fascism, he wanted to know, all those green people plotting to take over the world?

No, actually I was not. I _was_ alarmed, however, about not being able to go to the beach that week because the water had been declared unfit for swimming. I was alarmed that the federal government was unwilling to implement measures to curb ozone-layer depletion. I also was alarmed that the editor of a design publication was eager to kill the messenger rather than hear that the condition of the water and air was relevant to his profession.

Still, this editor did recognize the problem of reductionism in the environmental movement. Not every challenge that we face can be traced to an environmental cause. A park, for instance, is a meeting place for a number of issues that cannot be reduced to one set of terms. The abdication of government; the representation of cultural difference; the retreat of the rich into private, privileged enclaves; the transfer of wealth from the geographically rooted industrial city to global communication networks—all of these issues are germane to the subject of parks today. They are all major urban priorities.

The issue of the environment warrants special focus for two reasons. The first is the park's traditional power to evoke imitations of nature. Many environmentalists insist that we should abandon our traditional binary distinctions between nature and culture. I believe that the urban park may provide the most readily available site for reconfiguring the relationships between them.

The second reason is that the editor's attitude of martial resistance is not an isolated one. In fact, my decision to hire an environmentalist to teach a required course in the criticism program was controversial. Several members of the program's advisory board were opposed to the idea. They could not accept that a course dealing in part with scientific theory deserved a place in a program designed chiefly to educate people to evaluate works of art. After all, each of our advisors had attained eminence in the field of architectural journalism without this kind of information. Acceding to the need for an environmentalist, perhaps, would have implied that they were missing something important in their own view of architecture and design.

I encountered a similar resistance three years ago when I participated in a thesis review at the University of California, Los Angeles (UCLA), School of Architecture. Most interesting to me was a water-reclamation facility for the city of Santa Cruz designed by a student named Warren Wagner. The project appealed to me for a number of reasons, not least because I found it brilliant in purely formal terms. It possessed some of the lyrical beauty of the industrial landscapes one admires at a distance from a highway. Yet it was clear from Wagner's presentation that his formal moves had developed simultaneously with his research into the technology of water reclamation. It was also clear that the jury was reluctant to recognize this aspect of his work as a work of architecture. They saw it, if anything, as a major feat of plumbing.

Each year, UCLA provides several thesis projects that, in name at least, address environmental issues. But Wagner had moved beyond any previous project I had seen in developing a viable technical facility. In doing so, he had clearly crossed a line. He had moved into an area that his faculty could no longer evaluate with confidence. Although I, too, could not adequately assess the success or failure of his work from a technical point of view, I could assess the shortcomings of the educational structure in which Wagner was operating, and of which I was, at least temporarily, a part. I saw that our collective inability to judge him on other than formal terms was a significant flaw.

Since that incident three years ago, there has been a great deal of public discussion about the environment. The topic has been featured in magazines, pop songs, and rainforest rallies; even George Bush is on record as being worried about the thinning of the atmosphere over Kennebunkport. Not coincidentally, in the recent past, there has been a proliferation of books, publications, and exhibitions on the subject of landscape design.

HERBERT MUSCHAMP IS THE ARCHITECTURE CRITIC FOR THE NEW YORK TIMES. HE FOUNDED THE ARCHITECTURE AND DESIGN CRITICISM PROGRAM AT PARSONS SCHOOL OF DESIGN, NEW YORK.

One such exhibition, held recently in New York City, was especially significant because it indicated the extent to which environmental issues have become a major focus in the schools. Entitled New Park: New Ideas, the exhibition came about when the Municipal Art Society became aware that studios in five major design schools had independently decided to tackle the same project: the design of a twenty-one-acre park on the Upper West Side of Manhattan, on the site now developed into a park by Donald Trump as part of his Riverside South Complex.

That coincidence, in itself, was remarkable, as was the show, in which the level of formal and conceptual inventiveness was very high. Still, the exhibition revealed the same structural flaw that I had encountered at UCLA. There was a missing piece: the contextual information needed to assess what we were being invited to look at. Clearly, the majority of the students had ecology on their minds; more than half proposed to reclaim at least a portion of the site as a tidal salt marsh. To designate a strip along the Hudson River shoreline as a salt marsh, however, does not mean that the design is more ecologically sophisticated than a proposal to construct a concrete seawall. Ecology deals not with parts but with systems in which each part is affected by every other part. A park is at once a system of related parts and a part of other systems that lie largely outside its boundaries. We cannot truly assess the introduction into a given area of, say, a salt marsh without adequate information about these relationships.

Obviously, a temporary exhibition cannot offer the average visitor much information on the ecosystem of the Hudson River. Corporations with assets considerably more substantial than those of the Municipal Art Society have courted bankruptcy over the costs of preparing environmental-impact statements for projects located in sites that are far less complex than the one in this exhibition. Yet the show missed a golden opportunity in failing to communicate to the visitor the critical importance of this ecological information. Instead, we were left with the impression that the projects on view could be adequately assessed on the basis of visual information alone. The logic is not hard to defend; these projects were, after all, the work of design students, whose primary training is focused upon the making of visual form.

Yet this logic points to a deeper problem with the show, which is the extent to which the students were or were not encouraged to reach beyond form-making in their design process. Here is another example of the visitor to the show not being given sufficient information to address this question. The graphic representations of salt marshes and other elements indicated that the students had, to some extent, been exposed to information about the ecology of the river. Still, how were we to judge whether these graphic devices were anything other than green packaging—the very kind of deceptive sales practices consumers are warned about? At Parsons School of Design, which is where I teach and which was one of the five schools represented, there was only minimal access to environmental knowledge and no real requirement that it be incorporated into the design process. Perhaps some of the schools offered more information, perhaps less. Whatever the case, the exhibition gave us no opportunity to observe this, much less to grasp the differences between landscape training that is more closely allied to forestry and horticulture and that which more nearly resembles architecture. What we saw, instead, was a series of landscape designs presented as though they were landscape paintings. What we saw, in other words, was a classic example of the hegemony of visual culture—of the dominance of visual images over other kinds of content. If there is one place where that hegemony should be challenged, it is in the design of new parks. We need to know not only how parks look but also how they work.

Coincidentally, I was recently invited to act as an unofficial advisor to the team officially commissioned to design the park for the Trump site. As the project proceeded, it became evident that it suffered from the same structural problem that marked the show of student work. Somehow, funds had been made available to pay visual artists to work together on this project. But no money was initially offered to retain as a team member someone who could serve as a source of environmental knowledge. While the Riverside South organization did ask me and a few environmental experts for advice on environmental matters, we were unpaid and played no significant role in the process of design development. At meetings in which we were given the opportunity to comment on the design, the environmentalists were on occasion angry that so little regard was given to their area of concern. Perhaps their anger is evidence of eco-fascism. To me, it was evidence of the flawed hierarchical structure that positions artists as enlightened gurus and environmentalists as town complainers.

Why had the team been configured as a hierarchy that set visual culture at the apex and environmental information at the bottom in the form of unpaid volunteerism? In the best situation, environmentalists are paid technical support brought in after the design is completed to implement visual forms and make them work.

The history of landscape design sheds some light on this issue. Landscape is itself a visual concept. It marks the conversion of land into a source of imagery. We can trace this conversion to the architects of Italian villas who, in the Renaissance, took a strong hand in transforming farmland into picturesque settings for aristocratic lives. In effect, they transformed agriculture into visual culture, a legacy that lives on in the great urban parks of the nineteenth century and in the small squares of green lawn laid down over desert or swamp terrains as symbols of liberation from urban congestion. While this legacy has been environmentally harmful, its sociological benefits have been profound. The abstraction of landscape from land has been, in part, a feature of democratization, providing many with open space and contact with at least an ideal of the natural.

The Romantic legacy of the artist is another element in the structure of visual hegemony. The design of parks also implies the Romantic image of the artist as someone who is uniquely attuned to nature's harmonies, unfettered by artifice and the compromise of civilization. Although one might think that this stereotype was obsolete, it returned in the 1980s, a decade when art, particularly contemporary art, was often called upon to sanctify the inflated material acquisitiveness of the period. Perhaps nowhere was this more conspicuous than in the field of public art. Here, artists were asked to support the illusion that the public stood to gain from public art projects. In fact, such projects often robbed the public, since they resulted from so-called public-private partnerships in which the public sector abdicated responsibility to private enterprise.

The major factor contributing to the primacy of visual form in park design is the specialization that marks all of our cultural life. Design schools are specialized, as are design firms. Although we envisage artists in a Romantic sense as conceptualizers whose abilities transcend compartmentalization, they, too, operate in a specialized field. Public artists emerged in the 1980s as a specialty within the specialty of contemporary art—a group of individuals who, despite the sometimes dubious economics that made their work possible, have nonetheless produced some of the most significant work of our time.

I myself am a specialist, and, as a critic, I like to think that I am on the side of art. If I am sometimes harshly critical of the structures in which artists today often find themselves, that is not because I do not respect the work of the artists themselves. Rather, I think the flaws in these structures have compromised the integrity of that work. Art itself is made to look ridiculous when artists are called upon to perform outside their area of competence. The problem with the garden designed by Jennifer Bartlett for Battery Park City in 1989, for instance, was not only its environmental insensitivity but also that her insensitivity called forth the public's latent hostility toward art. It appeared to justify the public's demand that artists be restricted.

Nothing could be more unfortunate, for what is extraordinary about parks today is the enormous opportunity they represent for artists to work in new ways. If specialization is the pivotal problem, then I believe parks can provide a pivotal solution, precisely because they can bring together in one site individuals from the most diverse range of specialized disciplines. Perhaps no other type of project today offers a more concentrated opportunity for specialists to experiment with the possibilities of cross-disciplinary design. Most people accept that the hallmark of urban parks today is their rich cultural and social diversity. Their design can also be a meeting ground for diverse and contradictory ways of thinking. Park officials speak of "desire lines"—those tracks that become marked in the landscape by the feet of those who leave the official pathways. The design of a park should also bear the traces of unrestricted exchange between ordinarily segregated fields of knowledge. As such, they can become models for cross-disciplinary collaboration elsewhere. The architect Emilo Ambasz has described the garden as a place for the "myth of beginnings." This need not mean that gardens and parks should be designed to recall some ancient Arcadia. They can also be points of departure for developing new approaches to design—experiments in cultural as well as environmental ecology.

But how to begin? While the prospect of cross-disciplinary design may be inspiring, the fact is that we are not there yet. Somehow, a team of bright, informed, idealistic people can still band together and not notice that a player is missing from the team. Why? All of us are bombarded by the same information about ozone and toxicity; clearly there is no lack of information. Why, then, isn't it getting through?

The question is one that goes well beyond environmental issues to enter the complex realm of human behavior. At the risk of seeming like an "eco-fascist" myself, I would like to locate some clues in a classic study of the most extreme case of social inaction in the face of catastrophe.

In his book *The Terrible Secret: Suppression of the Truth about Hitler's Final Solution* (1982), the historian Walter Laqueur tries to fathom the inadequacy of responses to the genocide of European Jewry. He asks not only, "What was known?" but also, "Why was it not believed?" For, as he documents, information about Hitler's machinery for annihilation was widely available in Europe and beyond a full three years before the end of the war and the liberation of the death camps.

Laqueur writes, "The problem was put most succinctly by [Supreme Court Justice] Felix Frankfurter in a meeting during the war with Jan Karski, a Polish emissary recently arrived, who told him about the mass slaughter in Europe. Frankfurter told Karski that he did not believe him. When Karski protested, Frankfurter explained that he did not imply that Karski had in any way not told the truth, he simply meant that he could not believe him—there was a difference."

"What is the reason," Laqueur asks, "for the inclination among otherwise normal, even highly intelligent human beings to deny reality, however glaring? Clearly, it is a question of judgment rather than intellect. Judgment can be affected by a great many factors: ideological prejudice may be so strong as to exclude all 'unwelcome information'; a mood, such as unwarranted optimism or pessimism may influence it."

What kind of judgment produced two advertisements that appeared in a recent issue of *The New Yorker*? Both were marketing fashionable hats as a way of coping with the environmental problem of ozone-layer depletion. One ad said, simply, "Fight skin cancer now!" The other said, "In these

trying times of global warming and increasing ozone depletion, isn't it nice to know you can do something to protect yourself? In this regard, we proudly offer the Campesino Hat . . . great-looking personal ozone protection, just $21, postpaid." What kind of judgments are formulated by those who read such ads?

In New Zealand, where I recently visited, this kind of protection is not a laughing matter. It is not even a matter of choice. Children are now required by law to wear hats and mufflers to school to protect their skin from the risk of cancer. Perhaps our disbelief in this case is not that we doubt environmental abuse. Rather, we doubt our capacity to act collectively to do something about it. Otherwise, how could anyone suppose that the ozone hole is a problem for milliners?

I recognize that it may be unsettling to suggest that the discussion of the design of parks should be placed in so apocalyptic a context. Parks, after all, are where we go to attain relief from modern pressures—not to encounter them. They are where we go to walk and eat an ice cream cone and stare at the sky and not worry about the phone bill and the presidential election and the prospect of an asteroid striking the earth.

My vision of park design is quite consistent with this traditional use: parks can indeed be places where designers, through their actions, and, above all, interactions, begin to lift some of the bleak and paralyzing mood of pessimism provoked by the subject of the environment.

This, I believe, is one of the compelling reasons why so much public attention is being focused on park design today. What happens in parks in the near future will have not only practical but also symbolic value, as a sign of what we can accomplish in the building of an emerging global culture. Of course, no single park is going to make it possible for schoolchildren on the other side of the world to take off their hats and mufflers. Yet the park can offer something more than a campesino hat. It can create a place for us to take off our hats of personal protection and engage in a collective act.

This essay is an edited transcript of the lecture given by the author at The Once and Future Park symposium.

opposite: View of student Warren Wagner's water reclamation and resource recovery facility, Santa Cruz, California (thesis project, UCLA School of Architecture, 1988).

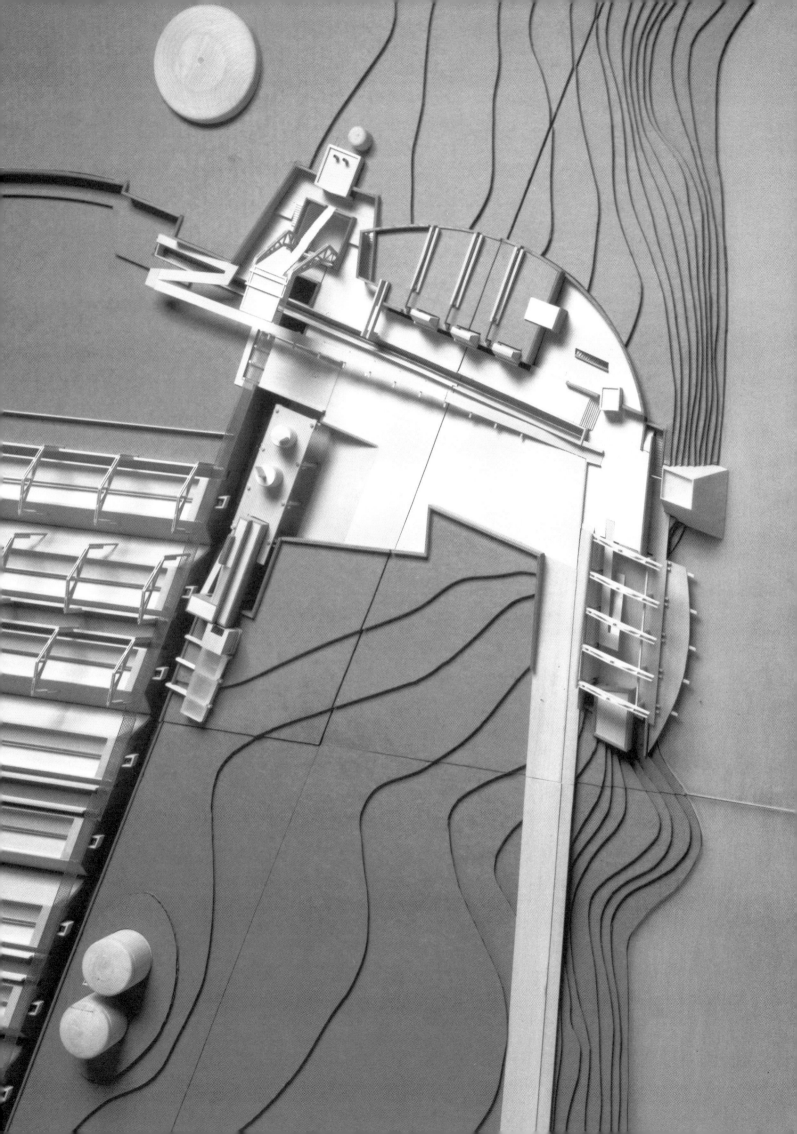

Public Park Inventions:
Past and Future

Sam Bass Warner, Jr.

In the middle of the nineteenth century, all American cities with more than fifty thousand inhabitants experienced a severe environmental crisis that involved overcrowding and disease. One positive response to this pervasive environmental condition was to transform the design elements of the English aristocratic estate into a municipal park, thereby providing a sanctuary for the populace. From then on, the large picturesque park, envisioned by the landscape architect Frederick Law Olmsted as an antidote to urban chaos, appeared in some form in city after city.

Today we face very different environmental problems than Olmsted's generation, forces whose scale is sometimes beyond our comprehension and control, and that require greater effort of cooperation and forethought. We have a superabundance of public and private open spaces, not overcrowding of the land; we have national and global environmental problems, not only local ones; we have a dispersed metropolis, not room and building overcrowding; and we have a commercially managed urban and electronic fantasy life, not an imaginative life driven by newspapers, books, and the theater. Despite these extraordinary differences, today's urban problems again require the redesign of what are largely private spaces into spaces for public use—not only reclaiming parking lots and undeveloped land but also rethinking the public face of private property.

The disadvantages of new cities in the 1850s deserve our attention since they throw light upon the intensity of the urban problems that called forth the invention of the park. The foremost problem of the 1850s was disease; no family was safe, and most suffered repeatedly. Behind the orderly rows of Victorian facades lay a miasma of sickness. The density of the American city then far exceeded the sanitary and housekeeping practices of its residents. Tuberculosis and venereal diseases were epidemic, and childhood diseases so raged that no city of fifty thousand or more could reproduce itself, never mind grow. Every large city required a generous supply of fresh recruits from the country. These early and mid-nineteenth-century decades are known in public health circles as the time of "the slaughter of the innocents."[1] Considering the incredible stresses on today's urban populations, this phrase could apply to some of our present-day behavior.

Like today's cities, those of the American nineteenth century suffered severe stress as a result of the demands on people's personal and public time. In shifting from the seasonal rhythms of the farm to the clock-driven hours of the shop and the mill, long days and unbroken weeks of work became the standard. Indeed, ceaseless hard work was even considered a moral standard for children and adults. The new textile mills ran twelve hours a day, six days a week, and masters expected their store clerks, domestic servants, and laborers to work those hours. The first American labor unions, bursting forth in these pre-Civil War decades, protested such driving of men and women and pushed for a ten-hour day and six-day work week. The Sunday ritual of church, a big dinner, and a quiet home was as much a rest from mental and physical exhaustion as it was a religious tradition.

In the 1850s, as today, American cities had a decade earlier experienced a period of explosive urban rioting and crime. Class, ethnic, and racial conflicts swept through the big cities. Gang fighting and property loss had become so frightening that cities imported from England that novel antilibertarian institution, the uniformed, salaried police force, who were ordered, first and foremost, to stop riots and looting.[2]

City dwellers then understood their environmental issues differently than we do ours. National resources were still considered boundless. In 1850 coal-smoke and water pollution seemed only nuisances along the path to progress. Urban public space in the 1850s consisted of a few old commons and squares, sidewalks, streets, saloons, shops, and hallways. Recalling such circumstances, it is not hard for us to understand why those Americans who lived in the cramped quarters of the time expressed such enthusiasm for parades and for the grandness of new construction, whether it be a monument, a new city hall, an opera house, or a railroad station.

Moments for fantasy, leisure, and imagination then, as now, offered relief from discipline and boredom. Americans then voraciously read newspapers and books, and they sought out the displays of giant scenic paintings, P. T. Barnum's freak shows, and the traveling circuses. Above all else, they flocked to that magic place, the theater.

opposite: Loring Park, Minneapolis, circa 1925.

HISTORIAN SAM BASS WARNER, JR., AUTHOR OF STREETCAR SUBURBS: THE PROCESS OF GROWTH IN BOSTON, 1870–1900 (1962), IS JACK MEYERHOFF PROFESSOR OF ENVIRONMENTAL STUDIES AT BRANDEIS UNIVERSITY, WALTHAM, MASSACHUSETTS.

It is against this backdrop that the city reformers William Cullen Bryant and Andrew Jackson Downing proposed the laying out of country parks in the as-yet-unbuilt spaces in American cities. The catalyst in this process, Frederick Law Olmsted (1822–1903), traveled to England, where he discovered his model for the city park, that of turning a private pastoral space into a useful public domain.

In the spring of 1851 Olmsted was twenty-nine years old, an indifferent cabbage farmer about to try his hand at yet another occupation, travel writing. For the purposes of his newspaper reports and later book, <u>Walks and Talks of an American Farmer in England</u> (1852), he adopted the guise of a farmer walking through England.

Arriving in Liverpool in late May, he immediately observed the city's harsh social and economic conditions:

> It would be more strange to you to see long, narrow streets, full from one end to the other, of the poorest-looking people you ever saw, women and children only, the men being off at work, I suppose, sitting, lounging, leaning on the doorsteps and sidewalks, smoking, knitting, and chatting, the boys playing ball in the street, or marbles on the flagging; no break in the line of tall dreary houses, but strings of clothes hung across from the opposite second-story windows, to dry. You can see nothing like such a dead mass of poverty in the worst quarter of our worst city.[3]

By way of contrast to this Liverpool slum street, he imagined a poor New York City street:

> In New York, such a street would be ten times as filthy and stinking, and ten times as lively; in the middle of it there would be a large fair building, set a little back (I would that I could say with a few rods of green turf and shrubbery between it and the gutter, in which children are playing), with the inscription upon it, 'Public School'; across from the windows would be a banner with the 'Democratic-Republican Nominations,' hand organs would be playing, hogs squealing, perhaps a stampede of firemen; boys would be crying newspapers. . . . There would be grog shops too with liberty poles before them and churches and

Sunday school rooms . . . by their side.[4]

The next day, Olmsted took the ferry to see the booming new suburb of Birkenhead and to visit its People's Park:

> . . . we passed into a thick, luxuriant, and diversified garden. Five minutes of admiration and a few more spent in studying the manner in which art had been employed to obtain from nature so much beauty and I was ready to admit that in democratic America there was nothing to be thought of as comparable with this People's garden.[5]

After the plantings and the pond, he encountered a lawn and playing fields where several cricket games were in progress. "Beyond there was a large meadow with groups of young trees, under which a flock of sheep were reposing."[6] Such scenes became a hallmark of the big city parks Olmsted later designed. Not simply foreign importations, they were also familiar to most American city dwellers since the pasture landscape existed throughout the northeastern United States.

Later Olmsted discovered that the park had been designed and built for Birkenhead by Joseph Paxton (1803–1865). Paxton was the head gardener for the Duke of Devonshire, whose estate at Chatsworth in Derbyshire was, and still is, one of the grandest aristocratic parks of England. Birkenhead suburban park, and his later design for the Crystal Palace Exhibition in Hyde Park, London (1850), earned Paxton his worldwide reputation and many imitators.[7]

Olmsted, admiring Paxton, heartily cheered the fact that the park was public, not the private preserve of a wealthy landlord:

> And all this magnificent pleasure ground is entirely, unreservedly, and forever, the public's own. The poorest British peasant is as free to enjoy it in all its parts as the British queen.[8]

While Paxton, Olmsted, and their many successors took the aristocratic English estate as a model for their municipal park (although theirs had paternalistic overtones), they also employed design elements familiar to the public: walkways for city promenades, driveways for horses and carriages, and an artfully manipulated landscape of pasture and open woods. To cope with the tensions among the classes, races, and ethnic groups, they provided consensus entertainments: ice cream stands, beer gardens, places to sit and watch the crowds, isolated places for lovers, band music, wild animals, boats, canoes, and horticultural displays. Few could misunderstand what sort of place the municipal park was meant to be: fences separated it from the street, fences and plantings directed people's steps, winding paths directed their attention, and an army of gardeners—plus a few policemen—admonished those who refused to take the cues.

Underlying these social and physical arrangements was a set of political and economic bargains. The municipal country park, located on the rough edges of a city's settlements, landscaped awkward fringes of land, turning them into areas suitable for high-amenity development by private real-estate speculators. Over time, the resulting increase in land values raised the municipal tax returns, which, in turn, supported the patronage employment of many gardeners and laborers.[9]

Today, however, everything has changed. It now seems infeasible and inappropriate to build country parks in cities, and the maintenance of the existing ones has become a municipal burden rather than an economic and political benefit. So new parks must play a vastly different role than they did in the past if they are to deal effectively with today's environmental problems and those of the foreseeable future.

Today's environmental problems consist of two distinct, but interrelated, destructive processes. Some part of our present crisis grows out of human relationships to ecological systems—water, atmosphere, and plant systems—and some grows out of human social patterns themselves. Our ecological crises are already forcing changes in human social patterns, but we do have many choices about how we may adapt to those demands in the future.

Our environmental solutions depend on limiting population growth and refashioning our agriculture, manufacturing, and marketing processes, as well as redesigning our cities so that they all consume less water, do not pollute the ground water, use less fossil fuel, and pollute less in general. It is possible that, over the course of the next three decades, we can meet these demands, without having to live in a leaner, meaner world.[10]

But the difficulty we are now having as a nation of cities in responding to our ecological crises grows out of our contemporary social patterns, and it is at this intersection of the nonhuman and the human environments that parks can play new roles.

The antisocial and isolating effects of the modern American metropolis have created significant societal problems. Some of these are discussed easily, such as the automobile driver's isolation from the landscape and his or her fellow human beings, or segregation and the hostility and fear on the part of the white population toward non-whites, the poor, and strangers. But rarely discussed is the underlying cultural system that has created these divisions, a system based on our psychological need for consumption and driven by economic necessity.

Perhaps the shopping mall is the best example of these forces, as it is the most heavily frequented type of public space. It is an expensive arena of retailing; an air-conditioned, artfully lit, theatrical space that we pay for with every shirt, compact disc, and hot dog we purchase there. The extravagant fantasy packaging that attracts our eye is also expensive, as is the newspaper, magazine, billboard, radio, and television advertising that makes possible the national and international marketing of so many of today's products. In contrast to the mall's extravagant expense and choreography is the commercial strip, any American road or highway along which we find the parking lots and buildings that have been brazenly erected by retailers. These strips are the noisy bazaars of our metropolis; they are cheaper than the mall for the retailer but are equally polluters and consumers of energy and materials.

For the metropolitan residents, the strain and discontent produced by economic necessities in some ways resemble the time stresses of Olmsted's city. In spite of sophisticated machines, our working hours are longer. Since the 1960s, working hours for employed Americans have stretched out so that we today work a month more per year than we did three decades ago. Paid vacation is shorter now than it was then, and more and more households have had to become two-worker homes.[11] The new machines, longer hours, extra days, and larger work force have contributed to our having more money for products and services. Ironically, however, the family wage today does not go so far as it once did because our living styles require us to buy more than we did in the past.[12] We do have more cars, more appliances, and even more living space in our homes than previously. But what sort of a life is it when our free moments are spent alone: 1.2 persons per ride in a car, one person per television screen, and a sense of sociability most easily found shopping inside the mall? It is impossible for most Americans to live comfortably within our consumer fantasy metropolis.

Americans are also experiencing an increasingly intense time squeeze. There is insufficient time to work, shop, drive about, do all the errands, attend to the children, and still have time left over for leisure.[13] The consequence is an extremely narrow and disciplined day, for adults and children alike. For children, from infancy on, life consists of school, some loose time before supper, then supper, television, and bed. For adults it is work, driving, errands, supper, television, and bed.[14] And the weekends? How much of them are made up of work? How much of them are devoted to errands? How much of them are left for play?

In the metropolis, the time squeeze and public spaces are inseparable. Today's spread-out settlements and dispersed job patterns require adults to surrender to commuting and errand time. And metropolitan time is now spent within enclosed spaces: within cars, shops, offices, factories, and malls. Even our consumer trophies signal our time and space confinements, and the absence of free self-determined time. The glitzy mall, the show automobile, the electronic toy, and the gated golf-club planned unit development—all strike me as fantasies of escape for tired people who have insufficient time and energy to express their own imaginations.

Surely the goals of a future park program must respond to the conditions of our current environmental crisis. Therefore, the first goal of future parks should be to help the metropolis build sustainable relationships with its water, atmosphere, and plant systems. The second, and compatible, goal should be to help the metropolis become a more sociable place for its inhabitants.[15]

Parks can help with both tasks. They can help provide relief from people's excessively narrow disciplines; they can present alternatives for leisure time; they can reduce the isolation of one citizen from another; and they can make spaces for people to exercise their imaginations. Parks can do these things by preserving patches of fringe metropolitan land for agriculture and forestry. They can offer alternatives to the automobile in the form of new bikeways, new walkways, and new minibus and jitney roads. All of these distinct pathways can be integrated with sociable pedestrian streets and shopping layouts—stores placed outdoors along real sidewalks and streets—and with fresh arrangements for the construction and management of the parks themselves. And such future parks and parkways could turn over increasing amounts of responsibility for their maintenance to neighbors and to the community and special-interest groups that use them.

In such a future program, park design and construction would move away from the beautiful pasture, sports facility, and picnic tables of today toward the creation of areas that would always be in the process of construction and reconstruction. Indeed, I imagine future metropolitan parks to be places for training and employing young people to work productively for the community as an alternative to today's all-school-and-television education.

One source of abundant open space for such a system, a source that exists even in the densest of suburbs, is the oversized asphalt parking lot that we continue to assume is necessary for every new store, mall, or restaurant built in our metropolis—at least two thousand square feet reserved for every metropolitan automobile (ten-by-twenty-foot parking lots). Only in a country the size of the United States could there be such an insane waste of empty space devoted solely to the convenience of a car trip.

Any town that wants to respond to the present environmental crisis could acquire these parking lots by trading unused city-owned land with private owners, then by narrowing streets, forbidding curb-cuts, taking easements for its new pathways, and by rewarding the refurbishing and rebuilding of its town centers.

I do not picture a single design for such a future park program. Rather, I imagine dozens being worked out to fit the differences among the many settlements that make up a given metropolitan region. To begin, towns could invite design teams from landscape architecture and architecture schools to hold a charrette that would demonstrate some of the

choices that are open to us all. Surely one of the special difficulties of our present situation is that we have few choices
offered to us other than the standard commercial packages.
But there are many alternatives, and, recalling the profoundly
innovative solution to our past environmental crisis, we should
be encouraged to respond with like inspiration today.

1 George Rosen, *The History of Public Health* (New York: M. D. Publications, 1958).

2 Sam Bass Warner, Jr., *The Private City* (Philadelphia: University of Pennsylvania Press, 1987), pp. 125–157.

3 Frederick Law Olmsted, *Walks and Talks of an American Farmer in England* (New York: Riker, Thorne and Company, 1st edn., 1852), p. 55.

4 Ibid.

5 Ibid., p. 62.

6 Ibid.

7 Geoffrey and Susan Jellicoe, et al. *The Oxford Companion to Gardens* (Oxford: Oxford University Press, 1986), p. 426.

8 Supra, note 3, p. 84.

9 David Schuyler, *The New Urban Landscape* (Baltimore: Johns Hopkins University Press, 1986), pp. 77–100.

10 Lester R. Brown, et al. *The State of the World in 1991* (New York: W. W. Norton, 1991).

11 Juliet B. Schor, *The Overworked American, The Unexpected Decline of Leisure* (New York: Basic Books, 1991), pp. 17–41.

12 Ibid., p. 111.

13 Ibid., pp. 129–132.

14 See the life of the Melbourne children in Kevin Lynch, *Growing up in Cities: Studies of the Spatial Environment of Adolescence* (Cambridge, Mass.: M. I. T. Press, 1977), pp. 4, 14–15, 21–26, 48–49; and William H. Whyte's remedies in his *The Last Landscape* (Garden City, N.Y.: Doubleday, 1968), pp. 260–270.

15 Sim Van der Ryn and Peter Calthorpe, *Sustainable Communities* (San Francisco: Sierra Club Books, 1986); and Doug Kelbaugh, ed., *The Pedestrian Pocket Book* (New York: Princeton Architectural Press, 1989).

Present Tensions:

The Nature of Public Space

Patricia Phillips

The past two decades have been disquieting ones in the history of public space. While social critics have decried the decline, if not the disappearance, of a meaningful civic life, the "mallification" of cities and suburbs has stimulated the development of commercial, often vapid, fun-oriented spaces. As one effect of this situation, many people nostalgically long for the past, while asking questions about what we may expect and create in the future. Now we must rethink designs for future public spaces not only in terms of a given site's spatial concerns but also in terms of its social instrumentality and how ecological issues are to be addressed in order to create spaces that are truly meaningful and socially inclusive.

In spite of abundant reasons for doubting it is possible, many still believe in the viability of an active and challenging public domain. As we consider new spaces for our collective activities, parks can play an important role. They can significantly influence how we think about public space by incorporating human policies, individual actions, and natural ecologies into their programs. By supporting the constructive tension between culture and nature, their designs reflect the many forms of conflict and adaptation that inevitably occur in conceived environments. In this time of difficult, sometimes dispiriting change, public space, and parks in particular, function as instruments for exploring philosophical and social questions—offering new concepts about the nature of public space and new solutions to their inherent problems.

Today, the concerns about a lethargic public life and imperiled natural environments provide a rare opportunity for creative speculation. Park designs figure in this speculative process in that they are unusual amalgamations of natural systems and artificialities, education and recreation. They embrace the challenges that individuals and communities face as they act and react within the world. Sometimes the designs are repentant revisions of past designs, such as from the nineteenth century, when, it is commonly held, people more consciously and constructively occupied the natural world.

Some of the world's newest parks establish a direction of inquiry that embraces both cultural conditions and natural environments. The issues that these parks explore will no doubt be adopted by subsequent park designers and users. By examining two new parks, both of which opened in the spring of 1992, I will attempt to explore the dialectic they suggest, which frames the debate concerning a cultural conception of environment—the coexistence of public life with natural systems.

One of Europe's newest parks, Floriade Park in the Netherlands, provides a fixed, unnegotiable point of view that keeps nature and culture estranged. There, visual forms triumph over natural ecologies. Nature is on display, and inevitable change is quietly suppressed. In contrast to Floriade, Papago Park City Boundary Project in Phoenix, Arizona, uses culture to revitalize an endangered environment. There, design is the point of origin that stimulates restorative change; the aesthetic dimensions of this public park are found in natural systems, not simply in visual forms.

Floriade Park was dedicated in April 1992. It was designed for the Floriade, a world-renowned six-month-long exposition held every ten years that features an extravaganza of plant displays and horticultural demonstrations. Cities and communities throughout Europe vie to host the blockbuster event, which this decade took place in Zoetermeer, a new town built about ten miles from The Hague. Its stark business center—corporate headquarters, hotels, and housing—has risen in a robust but ungainly manner. Zoetermeer, as any eager community would, fought to host the exposition, shrewdly anticipating the potential economic benefits. When the Floriade closed in the autumn of 1992, small areas were to remain as parkland, but major portions would be set aside as sites for housing and other new development. All told, Floriade Park is an opportunistic venture.

All of this grand speculation has been sown by a vast park for plants and flowers, stimulated by the representation of nature in a major horticultural fair. Every area, every moment has been carefully managed; chance and fortuity have no place in this park program. Designed over the course of ten years by the Dutch landscape architect Michiel den Ruijter, the park is touted as the landscape of the future. As disputable as this claim may be, the park is unmistakably a spatial and structural inscription of current concepts of culture and nature. It well represents a philosophy of design that reaches for an ideal condition—and then prescribes anything required to maintain the artificial, euphoric effects.

left: Rob Scholte The Colossus of Zoetermeer 1992 Floriade Park, the Netherlands

PATRICIA PHILLIPS WRITES ON PUBLIC ART AND PUBLIC SPACE FOR ARTFORUM AND OTHER PERIODICALS. SHE IS ASSOCIATE PROFESSOR AND CHAIR OF THE ART DEPARTMENT AT THE STATE UNIVERSITY OF NEW YORK AT NEW PALTZ.

Floriade Park (detail).

Floriade Park in final stages of construction, early 1992.

The Netherlands is a landscape of sustained tension. Its fastidious organization subtly recalls endless skirmishes between land and sea, where neither retires nor retreats for long. Vigilant water management, modest yet heroic, maintains a remarkable landscape, a concept of nature willfully shaped by human intervention. The underlying pressure, the inherent volatility, of this system is curiously disguised by a built environment of sylvan farms, tidy towns, and domesticated cities. Order is primary in the Dutch landscape; all the contention and drama lie beneath the surface or are channeled through a vast circulatory system of waterways and canals.

Traditionally, parks and gardens have been sites of imagination, semaphores of artificiality. They generally require constant management and maintenance. The park at Zoetermeer is no exception. It represents an unusually willful, flamboyant pursuit of unnatural occurrences within a simulated nature. The park does not represent the comforting aphorism "let nature take its course." Instead, it is an example of a site being micro-managed so that landscape is a preserved, controllable specimen rather than an energetic, unpredictable system. This not-so-subliminal park program is the "museumification" of nature. How its implicit message affects the visitors to this grandiose environmental and cultural program is problematic. To address the issue we must ask, What is the instrumentality of this new park? What perceptions and actions are encouraged by its plan and theoretical position?

While den Ruijter claims no particular ideology, there are clear formal and philosophical influences evident in his park scheme. The three dominant axes that issue from a common public plaza have dominion over the vast site. The scheme recalls Versailles and other formal French gardens organized around dramatic allées. At Versailles, the axes issue from a single point—Louis XIV's bedroom. At Floriade, each axis is a structural element, a column of vertebrae that helps support and organize all the viscera of the park. Visually, the axes are dramatic sightlines forming a discernible cartography for pedestrians. Within this ruling system, nature is engineered, poked, prodded, sliced, and diced—perhaps even quietly tortured—in the service of a larger philosophical notion of ecological consciousness, a concept based on aggressive intervention and indefatigable control. The park plan directs movement and delivers information to the visitors, destining their "experience." At Floriade, "greening" is not about living more modestly and responsibly, or pursuing more ecologically sensible habits. Floriade offers a heroic model where the "author" of a landscape claims exemption from including in his design the biological processes and natural conditions of the environment.

The public, like nature, is diminished by Floriade's spatial conditions. Its design objective is a finished product wherein nature is both the subject and object of domination. From a historical perspective, Holland's park of the future recalls the old and exhausted idea of formal Italian and French gardens. It conflicts with a growing awareness that the mastery of the environment is a dubious—often disastrous—ideal. At Floriade, both nature and people are restrained. Participation and perception are preordained; discovery is overwhelmed by didacticism. Floriade does not challenge or empower the public. Rather, the predominant experience there is one of awe, as the visitor succumbs to the surrounding spectacle.

While at Floriade, nature and culture have a contentious relationship, other historical models and contemporary strategies offer the possibility that park designs can exercise fewer constraints on nature.

In the essay "Frederick Law Olmsted and the Dialectical Landscape" (1973), written shortly before his tragic death, the artist Robert Smithson examined a successful historical model, Olmsted's great urban creation, New York City's Central Park. Smithson exhumed Olmsted's vision of a new urban park, which included as one agent in the design the public acceptance of a changing, evolving park, one whose molded character required the most extreme maintenance and protection. The longevity of Central Park is the result of vigilance by both park managers and the public who, on many occasions, have galvanized to protect Olmsted's supple concept. The viability of the park, more than one hundred thirty years after its creation, lies in its dynamic (unfinished) orchestration of culture and nature, of human policies and natural processes.

A park can no longer be seen as "a thing-in-itself," but rather as a process of ongoing relationships existing in a physical region—the park

becomes "a thing-for-us." . . . Dialectics of this type are a way of seeing things in a manifold of relations, not as isolated objects. Nature for the dialectician is indifferent to any formal ideal. . . . In another sense Olmsted's parks exist before they are finished, which means in fact they are never finished; they remain carriers of the unexpected and of contradiction on all levels of human activity, be it social, political, or natural.[1]

Olmsted's park involves complex, layered readings of this variegated site, ambitious engineering that revealed the complexity of nature. He saw the ecology of the park as substantiating public values in a city teeming with new immigrants. Olmsted's paternalism has received deserved criticism, but the connections he pursued between the public and the park produced an indispensable model.

In contrast to Olmsted's layered, topographical idea of the urban park, den Ruijter, in the Floriade site, is concerned with sign, surface, and style. In his analysis of Western society's infatuation with style, All Consuming Images (1988), the sociologist and historian Stuart Ewen uses the word "skinning" to describe processes and perceptions that dominate contemporary visual culture.[2] Everything—advertising, architecture, clothing, politics—is about skimming the surface, privileging style over content. But style at Floriade does not exactly take precedence over substance; rather, the two become one and the same. At Central Park, the image of naturalism was instrumental to developing a public life that represented a more diverse city. Den Ruijter's design, however, concerns the nature of image. The landscape—the park—is an invented image as artificially cultivated as anything one might see in advertising, on television, or in the production of a new corporate identity.

For the cultural critic Camille Paglia, this type of domination of nature, this need to identify and classify, represses a complete understanding of the environment's magnificent and menacing characteristics. An example of this is den Ruijter's superficially happy design, which masks a more complete understanding of human beings' problematic ideas about nature.

The Westerner knows by seeing. Perceptual relations are at the heart of our culture, and they have produced our titanic contributions to art. Walking in nature, we see, identify, name, recognize. This recognition is our apotropaion, that is, our warding off of fear. . . . We say that nature is beautiful. But this aesthetic judgment, which not all peoples have shared, is another defense formation, woefully inadequate for encompassing nature's totality. What is pretty in nature is confined to the thin skin of the globe upon which we huddle. Scratch the skin, and nature's daemonic ugliness will erupt.[3]

Thus Floriade, the superstar park created especially for a short-lived event, does embrace a particular vision of a future park, and it is successful in terms of pure pleasure. But however seductive its packaging, inflated to meet the exposition's commercial expectations, a design based on marketing principles may not provide the best model for our park of the future.

Is it possible, then, to imagine a park without a direct entrepreneurial cause? Or have parks also become malls? Is there still a desire, purpose, and place for parks when no marketing potential is perceived, no verifiable profit is forecasted? Do parks still provide people with something that no other situation offers? Rather than staking out specific sites and locations called "the park," a new concept of park may emphasize the instrumentality or role of parks and the distinct experience that parks engender. Perhaps the lesson of Floriade (a tired model in new clothes) is that designers and the public need to broaden their conceptions and deepen their expectations of parks, which would enhance the park's instrumentality as part of a larger agenda and encourage intimate involvement in public life.

Instrumentality is a key concept. Because of the hybrid nature of today's park programs and how they cope with issues of culture and nature, parks are instruments for discovering constructive new arrangements of social values and environmental concerns. In spite of the jarring fragmentation of public life, there may be new situations for public spaces and urban systems as part of a community's cultural agenda. For example, Wendy Feuer, Director of Arts for Transit and Facilities Design for the Metropolitan Transit Authority in New York City, describes the city's subway system as an urban,

cultural park. It forms a great subterranean sinew where people can excavate urban ideas and local histories. As a new model and strategy, the contemporary—and future—idea of park could suggest forms such as this one that transcend centralized locations and surpass discrete boundaries. In this way, parks provide mental landscapes; they stimulate ideas that extend symbolically beyond a specific place.

Intimacy is another key concept. Today's inversion—and confusion—of public and private geographies may allow people to make personal commitments to the collective domain. Home was once a sanctuary—a respite from a cacophonous public domain. Public and private were interdependent but spatially discrete domains. But with the advent of information technologies, the world and its problems have

top: Papago Park City Boundary Project water-harvesting system (detail).
bottom: Papago Park City Boundary Project channels and terraces (detail).

reached into the home and into private relationships and thoughts. They can touch the individual in even guarded moments of privacy through radio, television, and video. While the home has been invaded in this way, we should explore how intimacy of a different type then can become possible in public space. This intimacy includes the physicality of gathering publicly with others; it may also denote a psychological and intellectual intimacy with the world—a focused interest in how the world works, and in how we develop a meaningful relationship to the public realm. While intimacy has been displaced from the home, it may find new immediacy in public space.

These observations suggest that the idea of the park need not become obsolete but that the typology must be reconceived more generously and speculatively. Instrumentality and intimacy suggest a new structure for creative development.

In 1992 Phoenix dedicated the Papago Park City Boundary Project, a collaborative design by the artist Jody Pinto and the landscape architect Steve Martino. Compared to Floriade, its site and scale are modest, but it offers a powerful alternative strategy of park-making. Smithson, in his essay, acknowledged the artificiality of his dialectic, while seeing its usefulness as an intellectual device. Floriade and Papago invite a similarly dichotomous analysis. Floriade, constructed in the watery environment of the Netherlands, constitutes a pointed contrast to Papago Park, sited in the arid desert of Arizona. The design concepts and methodologies of these present and future parks also represent extremes.

Pinto and Martino embraced a damaged site, a dying ecology. For years, new growth had been stymied by careless recreation, development, and other interventions that diverted water from the site. The received program for the project was at once ambitious and modest. The site, an overlooked area circumscribed by major highways, was conceived to mark a gateway to Papago and local communities. It also was to serve as a boundary for the cities of Phoenix, Scottsdale, Tempe, and the ancient Native American ruins of Casa Grande and Squaw Peak. In their concept, Pinto and Martino addressed the issue of boundary, challenging its divisiveness and heralding its connective significance. Thus, Papago Park conjoins diverse communities and conceptions of park.

Like Floriade, the Papago project began with a challenging site and employed an axial organization. Unlike the Dutch project, however, Phoenix's park uses points rather than pattern. This episodic arrangement of points—either marking celestial events or pointing to surrounding cities—establishes an open-ended field of exploration. Axis is implied by tall cairns that record the summer solstice and mark the directions of both contemporary and historic settlements—reminders of the history and future of site management and human perception. How one is to view the park is not dogmatically inscribed for the visitor as at Floriade but rather is suggested, almost incidentally, through Papago's schematic organization.

Papago's primary installation is a structural system based, not on an orthogonal grid and skewed sightlines, but on the requirements of a challenging natural environment. Martino and Pinto developed a large treelike structure of raised rock walls that create seven water-harvesting pools. When there is an infrequent, desperately desired torrential rainstorm, water travels by gravity through the central "trunk" or channel and is distributed to the seven branches. The branches are rock terraces that form pools where excess water can collect and slowly saturate the desert. The contemporary landscape architecture of the Papago project employs an ancient technique of water conservation and distribution that initiates a process of reclamation for the desert. Indigenous plants were saved and replanted, and native seeds were scattered on the site. The designers aesthetically organized and stimulated a rejuvenative environment; now there are signs of recovery in a desert park that will change over time as a consequence of their design. Papago is not an example of a landscape or park as a fixed idea. It accepts change and encourages repeated intimate participation.

Floriade uses an extravagant horticultural model of park design. Papago employs a simple agricultural strategy. Both park programs share the objectives of environmental awareness and ecological education. Floriade pursues these goals through extreme order and didacticism. The site is punctuated with video monitors and lavish displays that instruct the visiting public about the ecology of the site, how to walk through and experience the park, and how to interpret the artworks on view there. Papago, in contrast, educates in a quieter, more negotiable manner. Its terraces are sites and instruments; they provide visual information and serve an

Aerial view of Papago Park City Boundary Project.

ally have embraced the natural world and offered rejuvenation for urban residents. Central Park became the model for how the iconic and instrumental capacities of invented spaces could negotiate between the forces of the environment and the pressures of the constructed city. Space influences program. Whereas the major monuments and constructions of most modern cities aggressively claim vertical space, parks must accept the horizontality of landscape and the multiplicity of urbanism. They require agendas that are more inclusive, variegated, and communitarian. Although contemporary media technologies have affected the morphology of cities, our modes of perception, and our manners of existence, and have in the process shown a disquieting potential for creating absolute isolation, we need not see that isolation as either a sanctuary or as our inevitable destiny. We need parks to help us envision ways of occupying the world—to help us consider ideas that cannot be imagined in seclusion. A complex and mutable program for the park of the future can empower the public to nurture constructive relations of (human) nature and environmental (culture).

Hieronymus Bosch <u>The Garden of Delights</u> circa 1500 (center-panel detail). The tension between humankind and the natural environment has been a philosophical problem throughout history. It is a problem complicated by our ambivalent feelings about both nature and human nature.

essential function (preventing runoff of precious water onto adjacent roads) in a gradual rehabilitation of the desert community. Floriade's structure is autocratic, while Papago's is an advisory process. Floriade employs pattern as concept; Papago uses concept as an agent for change. Floriade is about linear learning; Papago is about prolonged inquiry. At Floriade meaning is delivered; at Papago it is discovered.

At both parks, there are significant environmental and interpretative strategies at work establishing different points of access and occupancy. Floriade's model is individualistic and unyielding. Papago's strategy is collective and dynamic. Floriade is someone's grand creation. Papago is the community's—and nature's—project to complete. At Papago, Pinto and Martino have been agents rather than authors.

Since the nineteenth century, public parks tradition-

1 Robert Smithson, "Frederick Law Olmsted and the Dialectical Landscape," *Artforum* 11, no. 6 (February 1973), p. 63.

2 Stuart Ewen, *All Consuming Images: The Politics of Style in Contemporary Culture* (New York: Basic Books, 1988).

3 Camille Paglia, *Sexual Personae: Art and Decadence from Nefertiti to Emily Dickinson* (New York: Vintage, 1990), p. 5.

To Theme or Not to Theme:
Disneyfication without Guilt

Edward Ball

In April 1992 Euro Disneyland opened near Paris, clearing the way for the implantation of the Disney design gestalt in the Old World. How was it received? Thousands attended the opening ceremonies; millions watched on television in the United States. Meanwhile, French intellectuals availed themselves of an opportunity to exercise a reflexive anti-Americanism. In the April 6 issue of the Paris daily Le Figaro, the critic Alain Finkelkraut observed, "Euro Disney is a terrifying, giant step toward world homogenization." Fair enough. But the writer Jean Cau went further, describing the theme park as "a horror made of cardboard, plastic and appalling colors, a construction of hardened chewing gum and idiotic folklore taken straight out of comic books written for obese Americans." Tant pis.

Disney Company executives might have argued that the Disney ethos was not an import to France; it was already there. It is possible to look at the Hôtel de Ville in Paris, a mannerist instance of an already excitable nineteenth-century official architecture, and be reminded of the various planned Disney environments in Orlando, Anaheim, and Tokyo. The rococo fantasia of the facade and the cleanliness of the sandblasted stone both speak of a Disney-like urbanism.

Is the relationship between theme parks and Paris deeper still? The world's most popular tourist destination is Disney World; the second most popular, Paris. What could this mean? Part of the answer may lie on the ground. Baron Haussmann, the mid-nineteenth-century French planner, bisected and quadrisected the capital with boulevards and axes, creating nodal points for monuments (including the Hôtel de Ville) and converting the city's former medieval labyrinth of ruelles and culs-de-sac into a readable, linear, and panoramic space. Might Haussmann's planification be a foreshadowing of the programmed environments, perspective views, and Taylorized traffic flows of the Disney theme parks?

A related American case comes to mind. I sometimes hear a strange observation about my hometown, New Orleans, especially a neighborhood there called the French Quarter (uncoincidentally, another tourist magnet). The city of New Orleans, which evolved organically in the eighteenth and nineteenth centuries with a great deal of coherence in architecture and layout, is occasionally compared to Disneyland, an

association that is at the least disorienting, because Disneyland is "like" New Orleans, and not the other way around.

Yet the comparison is not farfetched: New Orleans has a large measure of surviving architecture that has been romanticized in the process of its disappearance elsewhere, and the city's relative indifference to the twentieth century invites reeking nostalgia. Romance and recollection are key Disney ingredients.

Europe and the American South may provide a good start on understanding the progress of Disney as a multinational firm and as an implant in our architectural unconscious, but Japan seems to hold the truest model of the "Disney effect." At the Imperial Palace in Kyoto, out among the gardens surrounding the old emperor's residence, there is a piece of landscaping known as the "picture garden." The garden's hummocks and plantings around a winding stream lie behind a wall in which there has been cut a wide passage, forming a kind of picture frame a few yards wide and some seven feet tall. As one approaches the wall, the garden appears to the eye through a window composed of the wood beams of the passageway.

The design of the picture garden operates on two levels. First, there is its landscaping, the mapping of nature into scenery. Second, there is what we might call the meta-landscape, the garden viewed through the frame in the wall, which renders the three-dimensional area as a flat, planar image. The presence of the frame, in essence the act of quotation, seems to erase the careful labor of the garden's creation and maintenance, reifying them into a two-dimensional scene.

The crucial event lies in the relationship between the frame (the act of representation in design) and its contents (horticulture, the stream). This is a nascent gesture of "theming." The kernel of theming lies in the priority of the image over the lived, phenomenological experience of space. This predisposition, much discussed in semiotics and cultural studies, is not as pressing an issue in architecture and landscaping and needs elaboration.

In un-themed space, a tenement may be a narrow six-floor building with twenty-five apartments that house working people. In themed space, a tenement is a meditation on a tenement: it is a meta-tenement. A themed tenement, such as the ones in the New York set of a Hollywood studio, is

opposite: Arman Long-Term Parking 1982 Foundation Cartier pour l'Art Contemporain, Jouy-en Josas, France

VILLAGE VOICE CRITIC EDWARD BALL WRITES FREQUENTLY ON SOCIAL AND POLITICAL ASPECTS OF DESIGN.

HE IS AN ASSOCIATE EDITOR OF LUSITANIA, A JOURNAL OF CULTURAL THEORY.

not so much part of the built world as it is a piece of it that has broken off and is floating somewhere in the miasma of spectacle and visuality. A themed tenement is not a building but an evocation of a building, maybe only a facade that can be heard to murmur, "tenement-ness." The notion of the theme lives in that suffix.

Walt Disney cut the ribbon at Disneyland in 1955, yet the eighty-acre theme park had many precursors. At the turn of the century, Coney Island in New York and Riverview Park in Chicago were built as new compounds for mass leisure, undertaken with the same inflation of scale pioneered by the factories of big business. In the same period, giant trade shows, such as the 1893 Chicago Columbian Exposition, the Century of Progress Fair of 1933 (again, Chicago), and the New York World's Fair of 1939, revealed a new fragrant intimacy of showmanship and design. At the fairs, governments and industry arrayed their wares in ever more elaborate musical reviews and set pieces. Framed environments burgeoned: representational ideals such as model homes, new communications systems, and paeans to the machine were poised amid amusements and rides.

What lifted the early amusement parks and fairs fully into the twentieth century was their use of the fourth dimension of representation, narrative. The emperor's picture garden may have introduced the frame—the sign of the artist's "telling" of a space—but world's-fair culture used architecture in a rhetorical way. The aim was to persuade ticket-buyers of the rightness of "progress."

Before the fairs, architecture and landscape design had dealt solely in two and three dimensions. The facade of a building presented a flat surface with compositional problems to be worked out, as in painting. The city itself, following Renaissance planning ideals, was envisioned as a giant slide show, with each view frozen into a satisfying vanishing point. In park design, the English picturesque style can be seen as implying a similar longing for the two-dimensional tableau: an ever-changing succession of idyllic, natural, and two-dimensional portraits.

The two-dimensional design ethic, the idea that spaces might deny their three-dimensional space-ness and regress, so to speak, into a composition, disappeared very rapidly after the inception of world's-fair culture. Henceforth,

American Jubilee patriotic musical review, 1940 season of 1939–1940 New York World's Fair.

architecture and landscape could be expanded into all the dimensions, including the fourth (time). The design professions entered the realm of narrative and persuasion. After the world's fairs, design would cease to be decorative; it would become tendentious and political in character.

At the 1939 New York World's Fair, which Walt Disney attended and which prodded him into the idea for Disneyland, politics flowed through the fair's "World of Tomorrow" theme, a vision of consumer society characterized by convenience, plenitude, and ubiquitous technological stunts. On the fairgrounds in suburban Queens, the Frederick Law Olmsted idea of unprogrammed space, wherein the public meeting place was to become a kind of crucible for democracy and the mingling of all classes, is dispatched as a distant and implausibly primitive dream. In its place, we get a theme park and architectural showpiece that devotes itself to the marketing of the incipient consumer culture.

The construction of Disneyland fifteen years later completed the process of the politicization of design, its removal from the realm of ornament and commodity into the arena of persuasion and performance. To be in the crowds at Disneyland is to have a sense of what Joseph Goebbels meant when he said that "the finest art is sculpting with the masses."

The key to the theming process, perfected with Disney, is the relationship to the past, whose architectural features are mobilized to create precise ideological effects. It is well known that the Disney imagineers (as the company calls its architects) devised their meta-buildings along Main Street U.S.A., the core strip in Disneyland, to be seven-eighths historical or "true" scale, so as to make them toy-ish, doll-like. The effect is to turn the experience of Main Street into a tour through Plato's cave, the idealized American vernacular buildings poised at the sidewalk like flickering shadows on the wall.

After the mid-century, theming overflowed the borders of world's fairs and the Disney parks to influence the worlds of urban planning and real estate. We can usefully point to the moment of inception for the current ideology of the mercantile city in 1976, when Faneuil Hall and Quincy Market opened in Boston. These places, which retrieved eighteenth-century stone arcades from dilapidation and transformed them into a cheery shopping center or "festival market," in the language of the developer, the James Rouse Corporation, were a pivotal instance of history-writing with design. The market, designed by Benjamin Thompson Associates of Cambridge, presented a burnished image of colonial "pastness" blended with up-to-date, boutique-driven retailing.

South Street Seaport soon followed in New York City. Again the handiwork of Rouse and Thompson, the Seaport shopping center took old buildings near the financial district, retrieved them from their working-class heritage, and created a bourgeois enclave for specialized consumption patterns driven by nostalgia for some preindustrial period. Maritime themes promoted sales.

Ever since, the vanguard of American urbanism has been seized with theming. Also in New York, Battery Park City, a large office-residential-leisure complex on the Hudson River near Wall Street, is yet another island of themed urban space. The Battery Park waterfront, completed in the 1980s, is a quite self-conscious place, with lighting fixtures that appear to date from the turn of the century, park benches that recall the 1930s, and a quaint boardwalk. People treat the area not like a public amenity, which it is supposed to be, but as a tourist stop, like Main Street U.S.A. On a given day, streams of out-of-towners will photograph each other standing around on the rustic boardwalk, as though in some architectural performance piece.

An important corollary to this type of urbanism is the rejuvenation and theming of historical monuments. Opened to the tourist public in 1990, Ellis Island in New York harbor is a vastly popular museum and sightseeing stop. At the turreted, burnished stone building that houses the Ellis Island Immigration Museum, an exemplary piece of framed Americana, visitors regard the story of the "good immigration" to the United States from the perspective of declining American hegemony and increasing ethnic pain. Twelve million people passed through the examination room of the main hall at Ellis between 1892 and 1924; forty percent of all living Americans are descended from these immigrants. Yet museum exhibits play down the fact that Chinese people were all but barred from the United States between 1882 and 1943 and speak cautiously about the forced migration of Africans. Instead, this national theme park writes a very specific Euro-American history with design.

If we look at residential areas and experiments in town planning, the advances of Disney-like theming are plain. Seaside, Florida, built on the western seaboard of the state in the 1980s, is a town written, if you will, according to a seventy-five-year-old script. A "model" town, Seaside uses Southern coastal architecture from up to one hundred years ago as its medium, that is, the white middle-class vernacular architecture of the old segregated South. The town is proud of its own re-creations from that region and time: pedestrian walkways, picket fences, wood siding, and peaked roofs.

Seaside was developed according to a document written by planners Andres Duany and Elizabeth Plater-Zyberk, a Miami-based design team whose firm, DPZ Associates, makes a specialty of retrograde urban forms. In DPZ Associates' Seaside plan, the entire twentieth century has been written out of architectural history. Sliding glass doors are forbidden. Flat roofs are forbidden. Air conditioners must be blinded with outdoor screens. Wood is encouraged everywhere, except in exterior doorknobs and numbering, which must be made with metal alloys specified by the plan. Lawns are forbidden and overgrowth encouraged, to evoke the old relationship to land that existed before the suburban "lawning" of America. Most interesting is a stipulation requiring white picket fences around certain homes.[1]

One objection to this kind of Disneyfication, apart

Homes and water tower, Seaside, Florida.

from the Orwellian tinge of its enforced small-town Americanism, is a traditional liberal complaint, namely, that it is not diverse enough. It is very possible that Seaside is ethnically homogeneous, populated by a self-selected professional class who can afford to hire an architect to build a unique house and picket fence.

Yet elitism is not the main problem with Disneyfication. To return to Disneyland in Anaheim, everyone is welcome at the theme park—whites, African-Americans, Latinos, Asians, Jews, Muslims—so long as one participates in the circle of consumption. Seaside and its Old South values may evoke the dominant historical narrative of Northern European migration to the Americas (up to but not including industrialization), but theoretically, African-Americans are welcome,

so long as they share the same fantasy and walk down the same memory lane.

The real problem with themed urbanism is its nostalgic character. Seaside is the town as tombstone. What we see in it here is a creeping nostalgia for a period that can only be lived as a death mask. At bottom, the motive for such a place is a desire to restore social relations that have been superseded.

What characterizes all forms of Disneyfication is a yearning to evacuate the present. It is regressive, not progressive in any sense. Progressive design does not necessarily mean unrestricted development in the old style of the modern planners. There remains a kind of progress that can transform social relations by working to modify untenable conditions—homelessness, the collapsing infrastructure, the degraded quality of public space—instead of fleeing the present to some turn-of-the-century fantasy.

But even if the Disney Company were to abandon its cornices and stunted Americana, and even if the homeowners of Seaside decided to leave the nineteenth century and return to this one, the appetite for theming would not fade. The question of whether or not to theme has become central to architecture. The truest option is to try to create alternative theming: non-elitist, non-nostalgic, non-escapist. This would be Disneyfication without guilt.

Some park designs have already pushed in this direction. The Parc de la Villette in Paris is an intellectual theme park built on the site of the old slaughterhouse district in the northern quarters of the nineteenth arrondissement. La Villette includes the traditional expo-site things, such as a hall of science that celebrates technology, a spherical building like any world's-fair centerpiece. It also includes a landscaped section, <u>les folies</u>.

The "follies" are a well-known experiment by the architect Bernard Tschumi. On a long lawn stand a number of two- and three-story structures, some with stairs and doors, the lot of them arrayed on the grass like useless things, which is what they are. The <u>folies</u> don't sing the praises of science; they don't give you a place to barbeque. They don't do anything but just sit there and let you climb on them and move through

opposite: Folie P6, Parc de la Villette, Paris.

them and project what fantasies you might have on their discontinuous forms.

In their nonchalant thingness, the folies (big playpens for adults) are an early and earnest hope to create alternative theming. But the repetitiveness of the colorful structures, not to mention their placement in the midst of a giant government-sponsored ode to technology, ultimately reduces them to mere quirky diversion. Still, there are other ways of theming space.

In New York City ghettoes, especially those populated by Caribbean islanders (from the Dominican Republic, Haiti, and Puerto Rico), there has been a resurgence of building, not so much of tenements but of brand-new shacks. In East Harlem, the Lower East Side, and parts of Brooklyn, buildings are regularly demolished, leaving open lots. In the rubble, little houses (casitas) appear: squat, two-room, shotgun-style cottages with a porch. Built by neighborhood people, casitas are replicas of vernacular buildings common in the Caribbean. Painted white, with peaked roofs and screen doors, they are themed recollections, not of some idealized American South or of Main Street, but another sort of place.

Casitas share with mainstream theming a kind of nostalgia, but they differ in their social effects. They become clubhouses for their neighborhoods, places for people to remember, vantage points from which to regard the naked city in its vast indifference. Casitas provide some thread of communal and public space, often in areas with no parks. They may also be seen as a design rhetoric, i.e., as political speech, the casitas' deracinated and themed architecture supporting the validation of ethnic origin.

Although casitas work in compelling ways, the course to alternative theming does not necessarily lie down the road of eclectic multiculturalism. We should not place our hopes with a kind of architectural rainbow coalition that might reply to the monoculturalism of places like Seaside and Faneuil Hall. The idea of themed ethnicities presents serious problems, not least of which is the transformation of national origin into a form of masquerade and spectacle. At worst, it would lead to a themed Caribbean park next to a themed acre of chinoiserie or Sovietique restaurants, and finally to the conversion of leisure space into a segregated field of demographic ghettoes, each like so many typographic fonts.

What is needed is something more mysterious, more off-center. What if there were, somewhere, an open-air diorama that depicted a part of the United States, in miniature, before the arrival of the Europeans, and the same area after the period of development? What if, instead of a Colonial Williamsburg-like evocation of an idyllic American past, there were such a montage of past and present that inscribed history in a complex way?

What if landscape architects began to create themed environments of discarded commodities? What about a park made of old automobiles, or used Nintendo games, or high-top sneakers piled in mounds? Would this be alternative theming?

What if there were giant useless structures erected in every new park? Not a cute "folly" but something monumental. These non-buildings, five or six stories high, could be made more mysterious if they were locked up and reopened according to a random schedule, and if they included hidden speakers that played music or the rhythm of a metronome, also at random.

What if there were a park devoted to the ruins of modern architecture, a grave-site filled with all those abandoned buildings left over from the various world's fairs? Here the promise of techno-science would appear in its naked simplicity, as so much hubris and bombast, a degraded monologue that has come to a skin of peeling paint.

Instead of demolishing vernacular American buildings and putting up apartment houses, what if small buildings could be moved and recycled as outdoor installation art? Then, in place of Disney's cloying seven-eighths scale Americana, we might envision the full-scale reuse and manipulation of America's ever-changing middle-class culture, with parts of our aging suburbia serving as objects of meditation.

If these examples begin to suggest theming of a new sort, it may be something like the urban program described by Mark Leyner in his novel My Cousin, My Gastroenterologist (1990). Leyner speculates:

> Soon psychopathology replaced ethnicity as the critical demographic determinant. There were no longer Italian neighborhoods, or Cuban neighborhoods, or Irish or Greek neighborhoods. There were anorexic neighborhoods, narcissistic neigh-

The burned remains of Buckminster Fuller's United States Pavilion at Expo '67, Montreal.

borhoods, and manic and compulsive neighborhoods. There was no longer a Columbus Day
parade or a Puerto Rico Day parade. There was an
agoraphobics day parade.[2]
And nobody came.

One of the old "psychological" spaces of landscape design was the labyrinth. Here is a realistic, even more fiscally feasible model. Why not themed labyrinths for storytelling, confusion, and improvisation?

What about themed zones or neighborhoods devoted to psychological states? Could there be a melancholy park? A park enshrined to optimism? A cacophonous park, where the roiling noises of the city did not dim but were amplified?

It seems we've drifted some distance from the old Olmstedian ideal of unprogrammed space, in which the park-goer does his or her own thing under anonymous elms. Even more disorienting, some of our examples are plated with

ironies, while others have been borrowed from the history of Surrealism or similar white ethnic sources. But against the nerveless hues of the current theme parks, and living amid their spawn in "real" architecture, it's important that all instruments be made available for the interrogation of the built world. Otherwise, we may as well fall into step with Mickey and stroll down the single short block of our Disneyfied imagination, singing, "It's a small world, after all."

1 David Mohney and Keller Easterling, eds., Seaside: The Making of a Town in America (New York: Princeton Architectural Press, 1989), p. 261.

2 Mark Leyner, My Cousin, My Gastroenterologist (New York: Harmony Books, 1990), p. 17.

Park Redefinitions

Diana Balmori

In this essay, in which I am relying purposefully on concepts and not images, I am searching for the bases of design for future parks. I am proposing an exploration, to see if, from ideas, we can fashion a tentative outline of future parks, an outline that is at once conceptual and bold. In this endeavor, the first question we must ask is, Do we need such an outline? It seems to me that the answer is, clearly, "yes." Currently, there is a pervasive disquiet in the design world about the accepted vision of parks. Indeed, in some quarters, it is suggested that the word park be dropped altogether, so that we may think completely anew about open public space. In a time of societal flux such as ours, old forms may seem inadequate or obsolete. But discontent with current form should not detract from the accomplishments of the past. In the case of the space called park, its noble history should not be ignored or discarded, but it may need reinterpretation.

Part of the current problem lies with the power of the image invoked by the park of the past: that of the nineteenth-century picturesque park, indelibly stamped by the great Frederick Law Olmsted. So successful were such parks in their own time, and so well established have they become as monuments, that it is difficult to imagine any other images but these for a park—the Olmsted vision standing as a perfect fit of public open space with the cities and society of its time.

But monuments are not living organisms; they no longer have the capacity to grow or evolve or respond to historical change; parks, however, in order to succeed, must be

opposite, clockwise from upper left:

Frederick Law Olmsted. Central Park, New York, 1859. The American park movement of the last half of the nineteenth century, which strove to put green in the heart of industrialized cities, produced such popular places as Central Park. It served, and continues to serve, as a national paradigm for urban parks—even though it does not meet social needs as it once did.

Richard Haag. Gasworks Park, Seattle, Washington, 1978. The preservation of a former gasworks and cleansing of its polluted grounds are characteristics that make this park one of a new type in which the goal is to restore sites to health and utility rather than to create picturesque forms.

Herbert Bayer. Mill Creek Canyon Park, Kent, Washington, 1982. In essence, this park is an elegant drainage system for a creek, located in a residential neighborhood, that had started eroding the narrow strip of land left around it. Sculpturally formed detention ponds and swales slowed down the flow of water, making for a new kind of park.

Diana Balmori (designer) and Alan Plattus (consultant). Farmington Canal Greenway, Connecticut, 1991– (in progress). The creation of greenways—parks fashioned from abandoned transportation corridors, such as canals and railroads—is perhaps the most dramatic development in American park design today. Configured as a greenway, the park is not so much a destination as it is a "way."

characterized by an organic responsiveness. While noting specific societal changes, then, we might ask what fits our cities and our society now, and what premises we can assume for the design of future parks. As a step toward some answers, I will register significant changes in the six arenas concerning parks, observe some of the problems arising from these changes, and end with a broad outline of how these changes can be made part of a new design, integrating complex ideas with new forms.

These arenas may be identified as: Changes in the American City; Changes in Financial Resources and Park Management; Public-Private Partnerships; Changes in Programs for Parks; Changes in Available Lands; Changes in the Design Process and Players: The Collaboration Model; and Changes in the Relationship of Design and Nature.

Changes in the American City

The American city today is not a megalopolis with one central downtown. With the growth of suburbs, the city has changed functionally. It has developed into an aggregate of inner-city neighborhoods, and, as the affluent move out, these, increasingly, become neighborhoods of the extremely poor: new immigrants, African-Americans and Latinos, and those left homeless and jobless by a disappearing industrial structure. At the same time that the city is losing its manufacturing, and often its commercial base, its infrastructure is crumbling or beyond capacity; natural resources—air, land, and water—are all in need of reclamation. Transportation networks are in dire straits and cannot command funds for restoration and renewal. Finally, as a result of the hopelessness and lack of opportunity produced by the loss of employment, crime has reached alarming proportions—the present-day American city is no longer safe.

The impact of these problems on city parks is obvious; existing parks are under siege and need great infusions of money, which the public sector no longer has available, as cities face diminishing revenues and critical demands. But even with the constraints of changing demographics, fresh ideas about parks may be generated to restore and modify old parks and to influence new park design. Parks, once conceived as fragments of country in an urban setting and offering an idyllic escape from the frenetic city, can become lively,

DIANA BALMORI IS THE FOUNDER AND PRINCIPAL DESIGNER OF BALMORI ASSOCIATES, INC., NEW HAVEN, AN INTERDISCIPLINARY LANDSCAPE AND URBAN DESIGN FIRM THAT CONCENTRATES ON THE DESIGN OF PUBLIC SPACES.

overlaid places, "ways," which reach out to urban dwellers and offer a welcoming environment. Both within and without the traditional American city, new opportunities should be seized.

Outside the city core, a new model of the American city has emerged, called by various names, such as urban village, galactic city, or edge city. These names describe the phenomena of small centers spread out along a transportation line, usually a highway. On the one hand, this model lends itself to the concept of linear corridors that can run from one small urban center to another, fostering new forms such as greenways, or linear parks. On the other, this very solution is partial; we do not know if the model of the urban village, linked by linear corridors, will prevail, as it is based intrinsically on the dispersion allowed by the automobile. We need to qualify our new city with additional components that will mitigate environmental problems, make it a central point of arrival, and, by the use of systems of transportation, such as mass transit, integrate it within a region. The entire urban environment may thus be sustained by a viable economy.

Changes in Financial Resources and Park Management: Public-Private Partnerships

The financial straits in which American cities now find themselves have brought about an increasing dependency of parks on public and private partnerships. The private sector is seen today as the savior of public space—and indeed of almost every public facility. How much of a savior we have yet to find out, as collaboration between the public and private sectors has to date been limited.

One model to consider is that of Bryant Park, which recently reopened in New York City. A cooperative effort of the nonprofit Bryant Park Restoration Corporation and the City of New York, the project has gathered more than $8.9 million in foundation, corporate, and individual support for park restoration.[1] This effort, which enjoys a substantial annual maintenance budget of more than $750,000 and is annually supported by members of the Bryant Park Business Improvement District, has opened up the views to its interior, provided it with garden-type plantings, and has been carefully programmed with activities. Park leases have been given to restauranteurs, and two new pavilion restaurants are planned for the plaza to encourage greater use of the park.[2]

Yet we need to ask a question about privatizing our public life, our life in common. The new partnerships, while promising, represent potent, live forces that have the capacity to shape today's parks, influence visual forms, and, sometimes, generate a tug-of-war over land rights or over public and private management boundaries. Whoever pays the bill makes the decisions—aesthetic choices, programming, and use hours are then determined by a group of like-minded individuals, often from the same socioeconomic group, whose vision narrowly defines the life in common; with this limitation, public space becomes less public.

This is not to say that public spaces can be designed by—or for—every conceivable participant, but rather that programming for the design should be informed by a wider set of citizens than merely those who pay the bill. And this group includes not just the users but also citizens who can address the ecological needs and functions of parks and their possible new roles in the city's infrastructure: specialists in ecology, utilities, and transportation as well as horticulturists and social critics.

The difficulty of including so many players is great, and indeed, for some, eliminating large city parks, for which there are rarely sufficient maintenance resources, is one compromise. A recent idea, promoted strongly in the past few years and reflective of the breakdown of our social pact, is to concentrate on small neighborhood parks, created and maintained by individual groups for their own use, rather like the gated English parks and squares for which only surrounding residents have a key.

Yet the public clamor for open public space exceeds that particular, limited design vision. Widespread public support continues to exist for the restoration of old, large, well-established urban parks and for the creation of new ones of a different type.

Such support and inclusive planning are exemplified by the success of the nonprofit Central Park Conservancy in New York City, which gathered more than $65 million in private monies to restore Central Park; the reforestation of the eight-thousand-acre Fairmount Park in Philadelphia, which was funded by a $1.3-million grant from the Pew Charitable Trusts;[3] and the 1989 joint endeavor of the Plymouth Corporation with the United

States Forest Service to expand America's "scenic byways," thirty roads of scenic or historic significance in national forests across the United States.[4]

Certainly, the need for private funds for future parks will only increase. The sources of these monies, however, must not reduce or eliminate the public nature of parks. The responsibility for developing the blueprint for a life in common must remain in the public sector, for only through a participatory process can a new, effective social contract emerge. The best chance for fashioning a successful blueprint will come from professionals employed by the public sector, listening to a larger social sector but paid for by private funds.

One source of private funds could arise from what I will call the Productive Park, a new form eminently suitable for revitalizing established facilities. Parks are by their use and nature obvious and appropriate places for environmental restoration, which is becoming a particular necessity in old cities. Flood-plain rehabilitation, shore protection, sewage and ground-water cleanup are all examples of revenue-generating restorations to reclaim vital natural resources. For example, Seattle's West Point Treatment Plant Park, funded with $250 million in revenues from a state cigarette tax and increases in local sewer rates, sits amid twenty acres of trails, bridges, wetlands, restored beach, and forested hillside; it was designed to attenuate the effects of the expanding West Point sewage plant.[5]

The Productive Park, additionally, has the advantage of flexibility; it may be defined in various ways, ranging from transportation corridor to a place for the cleaning of contaminated aquifers. Its essential characteristic, however, is that it provides an unusual partnership between the private and public sectors or different public agencies to produce monies for the creation and maintenance of parks.

Changes in Programs for Parks

Traditionally, the program for a park has expressed the needs of the client, public or private. But lately, the park-user profiles are the programming criteria, regardless of whether users have articulated their needs, or whether these conflict or are irreconcilable.

Nothing can better illustrate the pitfalls of this kind of programming than the placement since the 1970s of amphitheaters in a great number of public plazas. The amphitheater became the standard "public" space: to serve as a place for people to gather, to eat lunch, and to hold impromptu or programmed events. Usually a hard, treeless landscape occupying a large public area, the amphitheater can be seen in many cities as an unused dead space, imposed on the program without any relationship to site and location, or to the possibilities of maintenance of public or private events.

However, I suggest that we may find a new direction for developing programs if we link the design of parks to the basic condition of landscape: change over time. If we abandon the old model's emphasis on the connection between use and program and envision landscape as an organic, evolutionary element, we may then develop sequential programs that adjust usage to plant-life cycles and environmental changes. Some landscapes, such as Bos Park in Amsterdam, have already been created in this way, and they need to be explored further.[6]

One advantage of basing a program for parks on this essential characteristic of landscape is that it can respond to changes in the human life cycle and in demographics, providing both flexibility and continuity: a park would have the capacity to shift its orientation from children to adults, to adjust to an aging population, and to accommodate, for example, new immigrant groups or single adults living in condominiums or apartments. Such flexible utilization makes this kind of programming most appropriate to an urban setting.

Emphasis on the organic aspect of landscape can also allow design to work with the natural dynamics of process and change. This recognition was central to my proposal to restore the garden of a Louisiana plantation for the National Trust. Originally, the garden, which started as the productive working yard of a nineteenth-century plantation house, was planted with young live oaks. As the trees matured, their canopy created a cool, shadowy area below. When the plantation era ended, the garden became part of an urban site; the new owner, sensitive to Louisiana's hot climate, redesigned the space as a shady, regional garden with continuous fronds of live oaks, their canopy reinforced by wisteria and Spanish moss.

My proposal for the Louisiana garden stemmed largely from the fact that a great part of the canopy of old live oaks had, in time, been lost. The cycle needed to start again, so that with the growth of tree plantings, it might permit changes in use and in character—from a working landscape to a beautiful, shady, regional garden. A landscape thus centered addresses the problem of fixity demanded by historical monuments, by providing continuity within a dynamic of change.

Many designers, however, are frightened by the idea of leaving the design open to the effects of time. Our present design attitudes try to enforce a fixed composition instead of one that allows for change. Much more effort and imagination, however, are required to design a specific landscape that will develop over time, a landscape that also provides for careful design, further opportunity, and known results.

Changes in Available Lands

A huge network of outworn and defunct transportation systems and public-utility corridors—canal lines, railroad lines, waterfronts, abandoned ports, utility rights-of-way—are now accessible for use as public spaces. Some of these linear corridors have, by presenting different parameters, already begun to change the idea of park, while others may provide opportunities for new forms of transportation.

Greenways: One space successfully combining both transportation and recreation functions is the greenway, a continuous, narrow, linear strip running through the city into the countryside. The greenway retains its function as a transportation corridor but also accommodates pedestrians, joggers, hikers, and bikers. Greenways, which now encompass more than thirty-one hundred converted miles in the United States, have been created by the demand of citizen groups on cities, states, and the federal government to purchase or give rights-of-way to abandoned transportation lines such as railroads and canals, and along remnant streams, valleys, lakeshores, and flood plains. These public spaces are quite different from the older parks: in their function as recreational-movement corridors between areas—urban, suburban, and rural—greenways join parts and give maximum accessibility to all; they provide humane, green zones weaving through cities, allowing people to walk to and from work, schools, or cultural facilities. Greenways are dynamic rather than static—not peaceful retreats but ways.

One of the chief values of the greenway as linear park, it seems to me, is that it addresses the problem of socio-economic separation, to which the new urban village contributes. This kind of park, which accommodates movement on foot or bike, might be a possible restitcher of the urban fabric, joining urban centers to one another recreationally and culturally, and providing for the continuity of a space in common.

The linear park, too, provides specific benefits, as it enhances the character and responds to the various needs of adjacent neighborhoods. It might provide an outdoor activity for people in a health dispensary or child-care facility, or it might simply offer space for educational and aesthetic activities for children, teenagers, or the elderly. In other words, an interplay can be achieved between continuity and locality.

Two projects in Colorado attest to the public's interest in having something other than the traditional park. The Platte River Greenway near Denver links eighteen parks with fifteen miles of interconnected trails. It was supported by the Platte River Development Committee, which, backed by more than $2 million in seed money from the City of Denver, raised additional money from public and private sources. The Platte River Greenway Foundation, established as a nonprofit, tax-exempt institution, ultimately collected more than $6 million from federal, state, and local governments, private foundations, and individuals.[7] In Boulder, the success of the Boulder Creek Path, a seven-mile, shared-use pedestrian and bicycle path regularly traveled by thousands of walkers, joggers, skaters, and bikers, has led to the adoption of the Tributary Greenways Program, which seeks to establish an eighteen-mile, off-street system of multiple-use trails within Boulder Valley.

In addition to greenways, other newly available areas have opened up our vision of what parks can be. Some of these may also yield fresh sources of funding for parks. For example, I have worked with the Architectural League of New York and the New York City Parks Council to consider uses for vacant, abandoned public lands in a section of Brooklyn that lacks public open space but is rich in aquifers. As clean water is becoming scarce in large cities, and as Brooklyn's most accessible aquifer had become lightly contaminated, we investigated the possibility of cleaning aquifer water with an air-stripping tower placed on city-owned vacant lands.[8]

We have proposed that the New York State Department of Environmental Protection (DEP) fund the construction of a park in exchange for the air-stripping tower, and at the present writing we are working with the DEP to structure this idea. In addition, we have begun a public design study to generate ideas for this new kind of park; the study, in progress, will be made into an exhibition and a publication in 1993. Meanwhile, the attention focused on the sites by the three agencies has brought forth monies to clean them up and to provide jobs for neighborhood teenagers. We conceive this park as a model for a particular kind of Productive Park; not only does it have an essential regenerative aspect, but it also takes on a new, transforming role, as in the Unicorn Tapestries: a magical figure and purifier of the waters.

Changes in the Design Process and Players: The Collaboration Model

The process of the design of public space provides another arena of change. Collaboration among architects, artists, and landscape architects has attempted to transform the design of public space by a shift in the players. While its results have been questioned of late, and for good reasons, this endeavor has been extremely important. Collaboration has brought about some changes and has much potential for more that are significant.

Still, there is general discontent about collaboration because, simply, it does not often occur. There are two reasons for this: one, in fact the less important, is the result of the composition of the collaborative team: in recent times artists have joined architects and landscape architects as participants. Artists certainly have been welcome additions to these collaborative activities and offer much, but an unfortunate perception has accrued to their inclusion: aesthetic superiority. While painters and sculptors are perceived to hold true aesthetic credentials, architects and landscape architects are relegated to the position of technicians. And as artists have become the first among equals, issues of control unhappily arise to defeat the collaborative process. While the emphasis on the artist's vision may be an understandable reaction to the excessive control architects have had over the design of space, this corrective may in fact defeat the collaborative intent.

The second, and more serious, problem is theoretical: it relates to specialization in each discipline, in both graduate education and professional life. Specialization is antithetical to both collaboration and a holistic vision of a public space. Sculptors, architects, and landscape architects find themselves speaking different languages and using different tools to think about and give form to public space. When one adds to the collaborative mix the interests of other professionals— environmentalists or social historians—communication becomes an acute problem.

It is a problem with a possible solution, though, given time and effort. My own experience with an experimental graduate course, which I taught with colleagues from the Yale schools of architecture, art, and forestry, may illustrate both difficulties and successes. Language was the first barrier; the method and means of expressing ideas, the second. For example, art students rejected the architects' use of the word design. Architecture and art students rejected the idea of a management plan that forestry students applied to the "design" of a landscape, or, as the art students called it, the "creation" of a landscape. Only when we explained that the management plan was a way of designing or creating a landscape over time did the forestry students' approach become understandable.

Further, the students were miles apart on even the most basic methods of communication. Models and/or measured-plan drawings were unintelligible to forestry students. Architecture students preferred drawings as a way of expressing ideas, models for final products. Art students explored ideas by modeling them. Forestry students, who dealt with the ecological issues of the sites, expressed their ideas in words and maps. It took a full semester of work to make the disciplines understandable to each other. As a result of this experience, a two-year program has been proposed to focus on translation and the bridging of disciplines.

Despite its difficulties and faults, the collaborative process is the most promising vehicle for the design of new parks. When collaboration produces teams that include ecologists, cultural geographers, sociologists, or historians, it can bring about a convergence: by this process design can be unified with the understanding and knowledge of different disciplines, so that nature and culture can be approached in a broad and profound manner. Certainly, our new understanding of nature and survival encompasses knowledge from many disciplines; and a human life is too short for one person to acquire the knowledge and vision of more than a few. Therefore, collaboration among different disciplines may be the best tool we have for allowing the integration of vision and knowledge in the creation of a public space. Collaboration will require, however, that those entering into it for the creation of a public space be willing to look with sympathy, understanding, and an open heart on the odd language and sometimes incomprehensible signs of the disciplines of others. If such an openness prevails, the model created to integrate different arts in an urban context may acquire a much more important, and perhaps indispensable, role. From modest origins, collaboration may prove to be the most critical vehicle for the design of new parks and public spaces. Form thus may tie itself to current, specific understandings about what sustains life and what does not; form may then best represent nature as we see it in our own time.

Changes in the Relationship of Design and Nature

Examining the quantity and variety of definitions of nature given by the cultural historian Raymond Williams in his book Key Words (1976), we can begin to appreciate the historical shifts in how people have thought about nature. As used from the eighteenth until the mid-twentieth century, nature defined a more or less unified "other": an other composed of flowers, insects, mammals, rain, fog, and clouds—nearly all but humankind. A powerful aesthetic of landscape grew from this understanding of nature, the Picturesque, which has reigned supreme from its eighteenth-century inception. The most important rule for a Picturesque composition has characteristically been that the work of the human hand look "natural." This aesthetic, perhaps the result of the pessimistic view of mankind that the excesses of the Industrial Revolution engendered among English intellectuals, diminished the value of human intervention and, particularly, sought to make invisible the work of landscapers. To a large public the work of landscaping was confused with preserving nature. It is not surprising, then, that by the early twentieth century, landscapers and landscaping ceased to be part of aesthetic discourse.

In the twentieth century—some pinpoint the moment

to the publication of Rachel Carson's Silent Spring in 1962—another view of our relationship with nature appeared. In this view, the human species was seen as an interwoven part of the natural environment, albeit a destructive one.

Landscape design, too, must recognize this twentieth-century shift away from the Picturesque. Such a change in attitude cannot be expressed formally by the mere use of rustication as those seeking the "natural" have posited.[9] Rather, while our goal must be the sustenance of nature, our premise is the acceptance of the obvious artifice of human design, put to work for nature or by it. We may, for example, design a beautiful windmill to pump up and clean ground water or, based on the study of physics, run water over a patterned surface to produce specific forms of waves. The results of our design, however, will acknowledge human participation and intervention.

In redefining nature we are entering the field of myth and seeking imagery that satisfies the soul by form, content, and meaning. If images can express a vision of nature that moves us and corresponds both to our present understanding of nature and to our spiritual needs, we just may have gotten our new definition right. It will not be Eden, though Eden reverberates through all landscapes, and it will not be the Peaceable Kingdom, for which we yearn. It will, however, be the place where we sense life, its brevity, fragility, mutability, and intensity, and its connectedness among all living forms. Herein lies its difference from interior public space: it consists in the living; it is built of and for living parts.

Conclusion

The outline for our future park may be tentative, but it is not unintelligible. It is one that can be based on new definitions of existing institutions and structures and that can make use of their potential. Acknowledgment of shifts in the nature of the city, in management, programming, and the design process for parks, and in the relationship of parks and nature, gives us the dots in the outline; our exploration provides the connective lines. A view of the current American city as an urban village produces new park concepts, such as greenways, whose linear characteristics can yield opportunity for new design. Similarly, both public-private partnerships and collaborative design endeavors can be further explored as tools for finding new definitions for parks—the one generating models for revitalizing older parks and linking reclamation projects with revenue production and the other, with a refinement of vocabulary, unifying aesthetic, environmental, and cultural intents. In park design, the establishment of landscape as a sequential form of programmatic design can bring about parks that are living organisms, adaptable to a changing society. Lastly, a conscious declaration of our present-day definition of nature, a nature which, unlike that of the eighteenth and nineteenth centuries, includes not only plants and rocks, rivers and mountains, butterflies and burrs but also humankind, may permit a design that makes life possible for the whole range of life forms.

1 Bruce Weber, "After Years under Wraps, a Midtown Park Is Back," New York Times, April 22, 1992, pp. B1, B4.

2 Jill Bonart, "Building the New Bryant Park," Bryant Park News (Winter 1990).

3 Martin H. McNamara, "Reforesting Fairmount Park," Landscape Architecture (September 1991), p. 26.

4 Heidi Landecker, "Public-Private Partnership," Landscape Architecture (May 1989), p. 16.

5 Kevin Powell, "Topographic Statement," Landscape Architecture (January 1992), pp. 36–39.

6 Bos Park, or "Forest Park," consists of 1,000 acres of woods on land reclaimed from water through the initial planting of fast-growing species of trees and followed by replacement with forest species. Bos Park's successful plan was adopted by the cities of Utrecht, Haarlem, and The Hague. See Ann Whiston Spirn, The Granite Garden: Urban Nature and Human Design (New York: Basic Books, 1984), pp. 196–197.

7 Ibid., pp. 158, 161.

8 A "packed air-stripping tower" is an assembly of simple machines that, through the contact of a small volume of organic-contaminated water with a large volume of contaminant-free air, removes trace concentrations of volatile organic compounds from water.

9 In architecture, rustication refers to the use of materials in ways that approximate their original form in nature, e.g., stones that do not have quarry-cut faces, or wood that is not cut into boards but that retains bark or the curvature of tree branch or trunk. Rustication is widely employed across the United States in National Park structures. Its use is justified by the view that it allows for closeness with nature.

Designer Statements

Nine Design Teams Speculate on Future Parks

In April 1992, the Minneapolis College of Art and Design's MCAD Gallery mounted a wide-ranging exhibition of drawings, models, and installations that presented ideas for parks of the twenty-first century. For the exhibition, five landscape architects and four design teams were selected by a review panel of landscape architects: Peter Walker of San Francisco, Diana Balmori of New Haven, and Roger Martin of Minneapolis. It was not intended that any of the design proposals would constitute a complete park plan. Rather, each participant or team was to think about the complexities of contemporary life and explore one or two interesting aspects of environmental, historical, or social experience.

For each participant, the exhibition offered a rare opportunity to dream, experiment, and explore ideas free from the day-to-day obligations of client or teaching needs. For several, the biggest challenge was to present ideas in a gallery setting instead of outdoors. Yet, true to their landscaping passion, a number of them <u>did</u> bring nature inside—trees, grasses, and rocks—to create sculptural installations. For example, Thomas Oslund and Catherine Murray's witty golf course featured stacks of green sod vividly set off by "sand traps" of bright yellow-orange corn seed. And visitors to Lance Neckar and Kinji Akagawa's quiet environment discovered aspen trees and carved-rock benches along a meandering pathway ingeniously made to simulate bluffs. Among the other projects on view were designs for unusual types of parks that included an open waste system park, an urban street park, and an illusion and sound garden.

What all the projects had in common was the way they stretched the definitions of existing urban and suburban parks with a view to making them more pertinent to our rapidly changing society.

Presented here are statements by the designers about their individual projects.

Julie Yanson

JULIE YANSON WAS FORMERLY THE DIRECTOR OF THE MCAD GALLERY.

Memento Mori

Amy Stefan

It used to be that a person would grow up in a small town and perhaps spend some time in the suburbs but return eventually to the place of his or her beginnings. Now people begin their lives in the suburbs. Can suburbs be a hometown? Are not cemeteries important for lending this sense of origins?

In exploring the cemetery as an essential park form in our society, I wanted to propose an alternative to the nineteenth-century suburban landscape park. Looking into the future, it seems unlikely that the great expanses of land necessary for this older form will be available.

This project looks at two sites, urban and suburban. In cities, outmoded industrial sites could gradually be reclaimed, first as growing fields and ball fields, then as cemeteries. In fast-developing suburbs, where open space is at a premium, why not create a new kind of cemetery, on a smaller scale, in which crypts and columbaria could be non-intimidating forms mixed in with the park? Instead of the insulated, endlessly duplicated landscaped cemetery, this could be a cemetery of abstract forms relating to the immediate surroundings. The cemetery park would both record history and attend to everyday life.

Memento mori. (Remember that you must die.)

Amy Stefan is the principal architect with Stefan and Associates, Stillwater, Minnesota.

Parks and Parkways

Ann Freiwald, Mary Ellen Weller, and Bruce Woods

Today's larger suburban parks are laid out in such a way that most users must drive to them, thus worsening the traffic and pollution problems already associated with the city and its suburbs. The smaller, scattered parks donated by subdivision developers are difficult to maintain and do not add up to a whole. Pressing environmental and social issues make it clear that a new park theory, and a new meaning for the word parkway, are needed.

The park of the future should link home and work, city and suburb. Our project explores a new method by which suburban parks can be structured as networks of neighborhood parks and linear parkways connecting one suburb to the next as well as to the city. In this scheme, housing and employment are connected by means other than crowded, unsustainable, and polluting highways.

Chicago and its surrounding suburbs are the chosen model; this is an area in which there is a commitment to providing recreational services to community residents and in which there are growing transportation problems.

Ann Friewald and Bruce Woods are landscape architects with Foth and Van Dyke, Madison, Wisconsin. Mary Ellen Weller is a landscape architect with the Fox Valley Park District, Aurora, Illinois.

COMMUNITY PARK
BIRDS EYE VIEW

The Open Waste System Park

Mira Engler and Gina Crandell

The traditional park is a stylized, pastoral landscape that offers the illusion of nature as scenery. Challenging this tradition, the Open Waste System Park invites us to see nature anew—as a realm in which humans play an integral role.

The Open Waste System is a network of parks in which our participation in the management of waste is as inevitable as our consumption of material goods. The natural processes of filtering, sorting, sedimentation, and decay all become visible textures in the landscape.

In one's own neighborhood the planting strip between the street and the walking path becomes activated with the routine placement and removal of sorted recyclables. The next level of the system is to be found in the parking lots of suburban shopping malls and small-town main streets. Conveniently located transparent drive-by bins accommodate dead fashions and dated technology. An adjacent salvage park offers otiose belongings. Citywide facilities, such as the coal piles of the power plant, the sewage-treatment pools or their wetland counterparts, and solid-waste landfills, constitute the third level of this park system. There, schoolchildren and visitors witness both reclamation and deterioration at work in a twenty-first-century park.

Mira Engler and Gina Crandell are assistant professor and associate professor, respectively, in the Department of Landscape Architecture, Iowa State University, Ames.

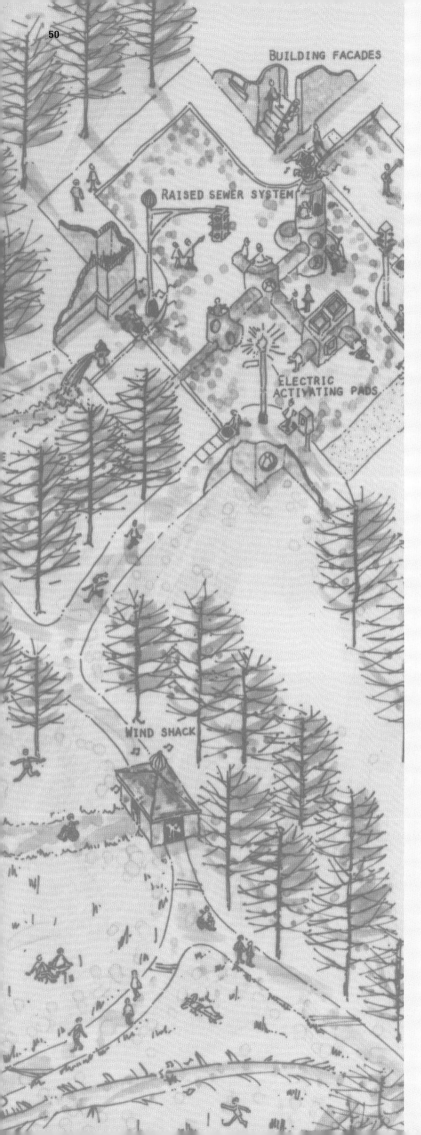

BUILDING FACADES

RAISED SEWER SYSTEM

ELECTRIC ACTIVATING PADS

WIND SHACK

Changingcomplex-
changingpeople

Mark J. Harrison

Can a park shape future values? Using current and future technologies, can we create intriguing park activities for children that foster discovery and accomplishment while building self-confidence? Such experiences would provide valuable help for living in a difficult, changing world.

Changingcomplexchangingpeople probes the lack of diversity in today's suburban parks, a deficiency that puts parks in direct contrast to the diverse, highly technological world in which we live. The resulting series of drawings and excerpts from group discussions propose creative solutions to correct this deficiency.

Mark J. Harrison is the principal architect with M. J. Harrison and Associates, Downers Grove, Illinois.

Ruins on the Prairie

Michael Koontz

This project explores the mystery and order of the prairie and the factory, using the poetic concept of the path. In the prairie, the path is a network of trails and bridgeways. The trails are narrow gravel beds that follow the natural ridge lines of prairie topography. All but the immediate trail is obscured by the tall grass and vegetation. These trails are intersected by bridgeways that connect the ridges, at level points, spanning the prairie's contour.

On the prairie, factories are generally built on the highest point of a given site, in order to minimize drainage problems associated with the flatness of the surrounding landscape. This makes it possible for the ridge trails to converge upon the factory ruin. Therefore, the shelter of the factory could provide evocative working space for the artist as well as space for a gallery.

The factory ruin is a symbol of an age of industry that seems to be fading into the past, amid the onrush of semiconductors and microchips. Perhaps the factory ruins are our pyramids, cathedrals, or memorials. Their timelessness, set against that of the prairie, can provide a source of inspiration for the artist and one of contemplation for everyone.

Michael Koontz is a landscape architect with Dean Sheaffer Landscape Architects, Dixon, Illinois.

The Missing Links

Catherine Murray and Thomas Oslund

We are so sheltered and comfortable today that we have lost touch with our place in the natural world. The token parklands left as (missing) links to nature are landscapes in a box, nature contained like a museum exhibition of organic materials. One prevalent boxed landscape is the golf course, the quintessential manicured pastoral landscape. In the Midwest, golf courses are often bound by development, isolated from the landscapes of the area or the agrarian landscape of the more recent past.

Future golf-course parks in the Midwest could evoke powerful emotions by using a vocabulary of images from our regional memory, such as the geometry of crop plantings, native prairies, or stands of white pines. These vignettes could link us to the region and test the limits of the game.

The exhibition installation abstracts common Midwest landscape elements and translates them into the golf-course fairways and hazards. Sod fairways become the vertical elements, creating small, challenging landing areas nestled between the corn-seed "sand traps" that refer to the agrarian landscape.

Catherine Murray and Thomas Oslund are Minneapolis-based landscape architects.

A Landscape Architecture of Confluences and Divergences

Lance Neckar and Kinji Akagawa

Bluff Creek meanders high and lazy amid a landscape of crops, woods, and suburban houses in Chanhassen, Minnesota, and then carves deeply through silty meadows and farm fields, moving water and sediment through steep hollows to the Minnesota River. The sheer height of its etched bluffs belies the fragile armature of the valley. These dissected bluffs and terraces set the stage for an archetypal park experience of enclosure and disclosure, in which the winding creek becomes the protagonist in the ancient play of prospect and refuge. The gate, the bridge, the path, and the shelter become allegorical devices in the evolving drama of hunting and finding.

The valley is a network of confluences and divergences. Each site of confluence or divergence provides an opportunity for a marking in the landscape. It symbolizes the notion that humans are not pitted against their habitat but are part of it. The markings provide settings for reflection, and they challenge whether our larger marks on the landscape, including the urbanization in the watershed, are in balance with the carrying capacity of the wider landscape. In this way the park becomes a palimpsest in a larger motif of ecological competition and succession.

Lance Neckar is an associate professor of landscape architecture at the University of Minnesota, Minneapolis. Kinji Akagawa is an associate professor of fine arts at the Minneapolis College of Art and Design.

The team on this project also included Gina Bonsignore, Perry Dean, Betsy Fitzsimons, Bob Gunderson, Tom Hammerberg, Erik Roth, and Jeff Timm.

Sensory Gardens

Marjorie Pitz

This project explores the concept of Sensory Gardens, a series of outdoor places designed to provide stimulation and relief from the sameness of urban and suburban environments.

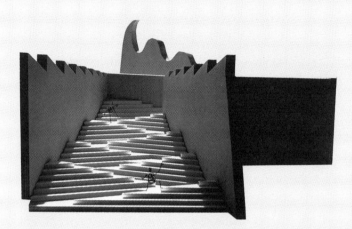

The Illusion Garden is intended to trick the eye and body with unexpected environments. Perspective distortion, reflective and transparent surfaces, mazes, and earth manipulation are some of the tools used to fool and surprise.

The Sound Garden encourages people to climb, swing, and dance upon a variety of sound-making structures that respond to the way they are "played." Music, sport, and creativity are playfully combined.

The Water Play Garden provides a circulating water system that encourages people to experience water power using whimsical devices such as water wheels, sluice gates, locks and dams, canals, spouts, and squirters.

Marjorie Pitz is a landscape architect with Martin and Pitz, Minneapolis.

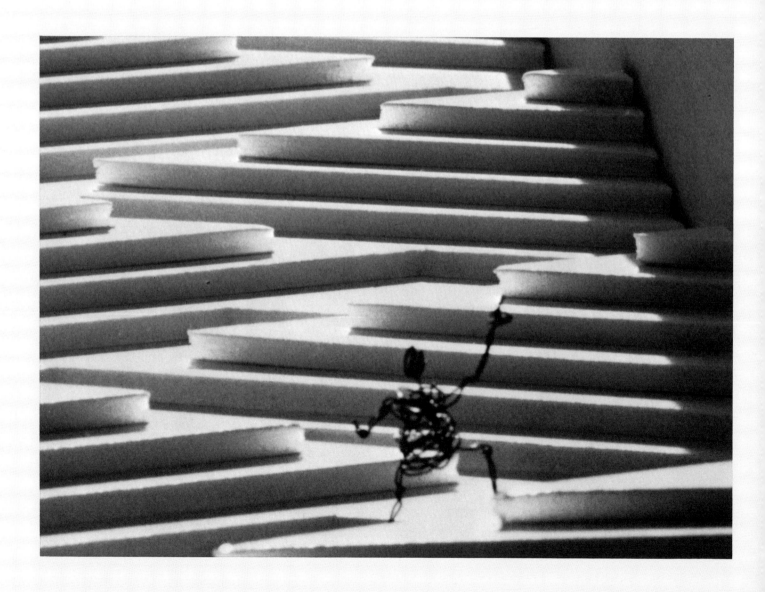

Urban Street Parks

Glenn Smith

Streets and Nature—two forces struggling to dominate urban space. One prevails through the frenzied interplay of automobile light, sound, and movement, while the other holds sway through the vivid impact of green carpets and canopies.

Americans often view streets and nature as locked in a battle of evil and good. This project suggests that a resolution to the conflict would blur the functional realities of the street and the aesthetic-idealized qualities of nature in the city.

Woodward Avenue in Detroit provides the contextual canvas for this synthesis. Texture is built up through the layering of iconic forms; these reflect how light, sound, and vibrations pierce the street as well as the surrounding landscape. In the proposed Theater Park, for instance, the symbolic automobile's "headlights" and its projecting light beams structure the physical form of the park. The Middle Ground Park symbolically echoes the sequence of sound, building to a high pitch at street intersections. The Cultural Park expresses a cycle of light and sound from day to night to day. All three parks are building blocks for an interconnected sequence of grand park spaces.

Glenn Smith is an assistant professor in the Department of Landscape Architecture, City College of New York.

Acknowledgments

This book grew out of the spring 1992 exhibition <u>The Once and Future Park</u>, held at the Minneapolis College of Art and Design, and from an allied symposium presented there and at the Walker Art Center; both parts of the project were organized by the two institutions. For help in realizing the project I am deeply grateful to the staffs of both organizations. In particular, Walker Art Center director Kathy Halbreich set the tone by leading us to choose an interdisciplinary lineup of speakers, which ensured that the symposium would be of interest to a range of professions. Margy Ligon, the Walker's director of Education, enthusiastically lent counsel and support; Education assistant Kristi Highum was vitally involved in every phase of planning and execution; and Walker editor Phil Freshman skillfully oversaw editing and proofreading. For their efforts in turning excellent symposium presentations into valuable essays, I am most indebted to the coauthors of this book; I learned much from each one and will always prize the experience of having worked with them.

At the Minneapolis College of Art and Design, Julie Yanson, the exhibition's curator, wishes to thank the following staff members who assisted: Brian Szott, MCAD Gallery director; Anedith Nash, chair of Liberal Arts; Susan Hanna-Bibus, grants officer; and Jim Becker, Lars Mason, Amy Ouradnik, and James Reid, exhibition preparators.

For their roles in planning the exhibition-symposium project, I would also like to acknowledge the assistance given by the three exhibition jurors, Diana Balmori, Roger Martin, and Peter Walker; the Minneapolis Park and Recreation Board; the Minnesota chapter of the American Society of Landscape Architects (MASLA); and the Center for American Urban Landscape and Department of Landscape Architecture, University of Minnesota.

Finally, my deep appreciation goes to the three people who were my collaborators on this book. Coeditor Steve Waryan and designer Kristen McDougall are not only consummate professionals but also delightful people with whom to work. And to Julie Yanson I offer my admiration and gratitude: she displayed humor and problem-solving skill at every turn, and I am grateful for the opportunity to have worked with her.

Deborah Karasov